"REMOVE NOT THE ANCIENT LANDMARK, WHICH THY FATHERS HAVE SET." • PROVERBS 22:28

An American Christian Approach for Teaching

CHRISTOPHER COLUMBUS

IN THE

PRIMARY GRADES

**BY JEANETTE K. SMITH AND
RUTH J. SMITH**

*To Becky,
Enjoy your
studies.*

*Jeanette
Whittaker*

Published by
PILGRIM INSTITUTE
GRANGER, INDIANA

(219) 277- 1789

PilgrimInstitute @juno.com

Published by
Pilgrim Institute
P. O. Box 454, Granger, Indiana 46530

Cover Illustration:
Martin's World's Fair Album - Atlas and Family Souvenir
Ropp and Sons, Chicago, 1892

Picture: *Pilgrims Going to Church,* Painting by G. H. Boughton
Used by courtesy of The New York Historical Society, New York City

PREFACE

The responsibility for perpetuating a nation's ideals and principles lies within the grasp of parents and educators as they show "to the generation to come the praises of the Lord, and his strength, and his wonderful works that he hath done . . . That they might set their hope in God, and not forget the works of God, but keep his commandments."[1]

Generations of children have grown to love and appreciate the unique individual liberty which has prospered in America as Christian self-government was exercised, Christian character cultivated and practiced, property valued, and discernment exercised in establishing and maintaining a form of government built upon Scriptural principles. The educational ministry of Pilgrim Institute is committed to assisting families and educators to place before their children historical examples of individuals used by God to forward His story.

Christopher Columbus was the individual Providentially selected and equipped to forge the path across an unknown sea, joining the Old World and the New. The thousands who followed after him planted the seeds of liberty which will continue to grow and flourish if the principles which produced that liberty are understood and practiced. Columbus's courage and character make plain the tremendous heritage of liberty which has been passed on to the rising generation.

i

TABLE OF CONTENTS

Table of Contents

PART I

TEACHING AMERICA'S CHRISTIAN HISTORY IN THE ELEMENTARY SCHOOL

COLUMBUS MAP.

ON THE OCEAN.

"The curious woodcuts . . . are supposed by some to have been copied from drawings made originally by Columbus himself. They give remarkable representations of the Admiral's own caravel, of his first landing on Hayti and meeting with the natives, and of the different lands that he visited." Martin's World's Fair Album-Atlas and Family Souvenir, C. Ropp and Sons, Chicago, 1892.

COLUMBUS

An Italian boy that liked to play
In Genoa about the ships all day,
That gazed at earth in child surprise;
And dreamed of distant stranger skies.

He watched the ships that came crowding in
With cargo of riches; he loved the din
Of the glad rush out and the spreading sails
And the echo of far-off windy gales.

He studied the books of the olden day;
He studied but knew far more than they;
He talked to the learned men of the school —
So wise he was they thought him a fool,
A fool with the dark, dark, dreamful eyes,
A child he was — grown wonder-wise.

Youth and dreams are over past
And out, far out he is sailing fast
Toward the seas he dreamed; — strange lands arise —
The world is made rich by his great emprise —
And the wisest know he was more than wise.

- Annette Wynne
For Days and Days
J.B. Lippincott Co., 1919

TEACHING AMERICA'S CHRISTIAN HISTORY IN THE ELEMENTARY SCHOOL

God commands His people to remember all He has done for them as individuals and nations (Deut. 7:18; 8:2; Joshua 4:1-9). Noah Webster stated that *to remember is to have in the mind an idea which had been in the mind before, and which recurs to the mind without effort.* Indeed, as Emma Willard observed, ". . . if we expect that memory will treasure up the objects of attention," it would help to acknowledge that "Each individual is to himself the centre of his own world and the more intimately he connects his knowledge with himself, the better will it be remembered . . ."[2] Hence, if the individual rejoices upon every remembrance of the grace of God in his *personal* history and world, he errs in forgetting God's Providence—His immediate, sovereign care and supervision—in his *nation's* unique history.

Today, the study of history has become a study of dates, facts, names, and events, with no consideration for their cause and effect. This approach to history has produced students who regard history as *dull* and *boring* and who have some knowledge of *facts* (or effects) of history, but no understanding of the *cause* of history and the individual's importance in His Story. Studying history with an effort to determine the cause and effect of events gives *life* to the subject.

The individual Christian must determine what is the cause of all events in his own personal history and his nation's history. Rev. S. W. Foljambe declared a causal rela-tionship in his Annual Election Sermon, January 5, 1876, "It has been said that history is the biography of communities; in another, and profounder, sense, it is the autobiography of him 'who worketh all things after the counsel of his own will' (Eph. 1:11), and who is graciously timing all events in the interests of his Christ, and of the kingdom of God on earth."[3]

Recognizing God as the cause of events of history will make the study of history truly Christian. How the Holy Spirit must be grieved when history is attributed to other than the true source!

A study of history from the premise that God is in control will cause the individual to recognize that God has a plan for each indi-vidual and nation. After Christ brought Christianity, Christianity through God's divine direction moved westward with its effect in civil liberty. This westward march of Chris-tianity produced America, the world's first Christian Republic established with a Chris-tian form of government.

In many classrooms, history loses its iden-tity when it is blended into a social studies course. The teaching of social studies produc-es an individual who has no mastery of history and who has a philosophy based upon man as causative with a great emphasis upon societies rather than the individual. As early as 1876, the Centennial of American Independence, Rev. Foljambe cautioned Americans against a failure to study Providential history: "The

3

more thoroughly a nation deals with its history, the more decidedly will it recognize and own an overruling Providence therein, and the more religious a nation will it become; while the more superficially it deals with its history, seeing only secondary causes and human agencies, the more irreligious will it be."[4]

The failure to teach history produces an irreligious people who attribute all advancement to man's efforts. History studied from original source documents enables individuals to see God's Hand moving to fulfill His plan and purpose and to therefore give God, not man, the glory.

American Christians must *again*, as the forefathers did, recognize that America is the direct result of Christianity and its relationship to all areas of life, including the sphere of civil government. American Christians must recognize the link between internal Christian liberty and external religious and civil liberty. If the foundations of America are to be restored, these premises must become an integral part of the teacher's philosophy of history and government and thus direct how and what he teaches in the classroom.

The directions for *Teaching America's Christian History in the Elementary School* given here have been developed for parents and teachers who already have some under-standing of the American Christian philosophy of history, government, and education. For individuals without an understanding of an American Christian philosophy of history, government, and education, the Pilgrim Institute offers a continuing training program to assist the individual in reclaiming America's Christian history, and relating a Biblical philosophy of government to every aspect of his life. (q.v. p. 115)

CHAIN OF CHRISTIANITY

History records the evidence of God's use of individual men and nations to move Christianity westward. This westward movement produced America and her Christian form of government. The links of the Chain of Christianity are the individual men and nations used by God to move the Gospel westward and the effect of Christianity in the civil sphere.

For further study of the Chain of Christianity, see *Rudiments Handbook*, pages 47-76, *Teaching and Learning America's Christian History*, pages 158-179, and their references to *Christian History*. For information on ordering these volumes and other resources documenting America's Christian history and government, see page 115 of this volume.

DEVELOPING THE ELEMENTARY CHRISTIAN HISTORY PROGRAM

The Principle Approach to American Christian Education requires the parent/teacher to prepare himself internally to teach America's Christian History in the elementary school through his development of a Biblical philosophy of history and government. Such preparation comes by reasoning, relating, and recording the explicit evidence of those Biblical principles and key links advanced by the Hand of God on the Chain of Christianity. The parent/teacher's own notebook will reflect his mastery of America's Christian History, and the student's notebook will reflect the student's mastery of that which is taught.

In *A Guide to American Christian Education for the Home and School*, Ruth J. Smith has developed a suggested program for teaching America's Christian history in the elementary classroom, which gives direction for the entire year's program.[5]

Nine major links on the Chain of Christianity are studied each year in the elementary school. These links have been derived from the more complete chart on page 6A, *Christian History of the Constitution*.

CHART A
CHAIN OF CHRISTIANITY

| CREATION | MOSES and the Law | CHRIST Focal Point of History | PAUL Christianity Begins Its Westward March | BIBLE in English | COLUMBUS Link to the New World | PILGRIM Seed of our Christian Republic | PATRIOT First Christian Republic | PIONEER Westward Movement and Falling Away |

Each link on the Chain is studied each year with the seed of the link being presented in kindergarten and expanded through the elementary grades. This allows the teacher to review the materials learned in the previous year(s) and build upon that foundation. By building the elementary history program upon expanding links, the student will complete his elementary education with a great mastery of Christianity's effect upon the domestic, ecclesiastical, and civil sphere, i.e., the relationship between internal Christian liberty and external religious and civil liberty.

CHART B
CHAIN OF CHRISTIANITY
Expanding the Links Through
the Elementary School

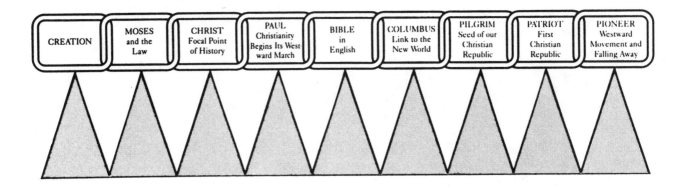

The question is often asked: How can the same link be taught each year without being repetitious? The goal is to expand each link through the elementary years with a diversity of ideas, thereby teaching without repetition. The basis for this approach is the Principle Approach to American Christian Education. See *Teaching and Learning America's Christian History*, p. 108, "How Can the Same Principle be Taught in Every Grade?" and p. 112, "Principles Expanded Through the Grades."

PART II

CHRISTOPHER COLUMBUS

Link to the New World

GENOA, THE BIRTHPLACE OF COLUMBUS.

("It was so beautiful a place that the people who lived there called it 'Genoa the Superb'")

"GOLDEN CATHAY."

The True Story of Christopher Columbus
by Elbridge S. Brooks
D. Lothrop Company, ©1892

— PILGRIM INSTITUTE —

CHRISTOPHER COLUMBUS
Link to the New World

History reveals God's Providential Hand directing men and nations to bring forth internal religious liberty and external civil liberty for His glory and for all the nations of the earth.[6] The United States of America and her form of government reflect the Christian idea of God, man, and government which developed in Europe and blossomed in the New World. Christopher Columbus was a key link in that Chain of Christianity, for he was the individual of courage, enterprise, and tenacity who opened the door to the New World. The opportunity and challenge to the American Christian educator is to discern the classroom methods and content which will most effectively convey to the students an appreciation for the centuries of preparation which preceded the opening of the New World and the contribution of Christopher Columbus and his unprecedented discovery.

Remembering its history has always been a major factor in keeping a nation true to its foundations. As the children of Israel passed over the Jordan River, the Lord commanded them to take twelve stones, *carry them over with you, and leave them in the lodging place, where ye shall lodge this night.* These stones were to be *a sign among you, that when your children ask their fathers in time to come, saying, what mean ye by these stones? Then ye shall answer them, That the waters of Jordan were cut off before the ark of the covenant of the Lord: when it passed over Jordan, the waters of Jordan were cut off: and these stones shall be for a memorial unto the children of Israel for ever.* (Joshua 4:1-7) The question which the children of Israel were expected to address for future generations was, What **mean** ye by these stones? As children are taught the history of Christopher Columbus, the question to be first considered is, What **mean** ye by these stones?

To answer the question of *what mean ye by the stones* which are included in the classroom curriculum, the individual educator must first analyze and identify his philosophy of history and government. The facts of history do not change, but one's *view* of the facts will be changed or modified by the view of God and His working in the lives of men and nations (his philosophy of history and government). The American Christian educator must interpret the facts of history from a Providential view rather than the current contemporary view. The individual American Christian educator must prepare himself by Biblically and historically documenting the Providential view of history and internalizing this approach to his study of history. A Providential interpretation of history will give discernment and the ability to detect error as materials are reviewed for classroom use.

CHRISTOPHER COLUMBUS —
AN INSTRUMENT
CHOSEN BY PROVIDENCE

As God was working to bring forth the *fullest expression of a Christian civilization,* Columbus was the individual prepared by God to forge the path to the New World. God uniquely prepared Columbus for the voyage spiritually, in the field of navigation, and in his own character. Columbus indicated this Hand of God in his *Book of Prophecies.*

9

"At a very early age I went to sea and have continued navigating until today. The art of sailing is favorable for anyone who wants to pursue knowledge of this world's secrets. I have already been at this business for forty years. I have sailed all the waters which, up to now, have been navigated. I have had dealings and conversation with learned people—clergymen and laymen, Latins and Greeks, Jews and Moors, and with many others of other sects. I found Our Lord very well-disposed toward this my desire, and he gave me the spirit of intelligence for it. He prospered me in seamanship and supplied me with the necessary tools of astrology, as well as geometry and arithmetic and ingenuity of intellect and of manual skill to draw spherical maps which show cities, rivers and mountains, islands and ports—everything in its proper place.

"At this time I have seen and put in study to look into all the Scriptures, cosmography, histories, chronicles and philosophy and other arts, which our Lord opened to my understanding (I could sense his hand upon me), so that it became clear to me that it was feasible to navigate from here to the Indies; and he unlocked within me the determination to execute the idea. And I came to your Highnesses with this ardor. All those who heard about my enterprise rejected it with laughter, scoffing at me. Neither the sciences which I mentioned above, nor the authoritative citations from them, were of any avail. In only your Highnesses remained faith and constancy. Who doubts that this illumination was from the Holy Spirit? I attest that he [the Spirit], with marvelous rays of light, consoled me through the holy and sacred Scriptures, a strong and clear testimony, with forty-four books of the Old Testament, and four Gospels with twenty-three Epistles of those blessed Apostles, encouraging me to proceed, and, continually, without ceasing for a moment, they inflame me with a sense of great urgency.

"Our Lord wished to perform the clearest miracle in this [matter] of the voyage to the Indies, to console me and others in this other [matter] of the Holy Temple: I spent seven years in your royal Court arguing the case with so many persons of such authority and learned in all the arts, and in the end they concluded that it was idle nonsense, and with this they gave up [the project]; . . .

"I am the worst of sinners. The pity and mercy of our Lord have completely covered me whenever I have called [on him] for them. I have found the sweetest consolation in casting away all my anxiety, so as to contemplate his marvelous presence.

"I have already said that for the execution of the enterprise of the Indies, neither reason, nor mathematics, nor world maps were profitable to me; rather the prophecy of Isaiah was completely fulfilled. And this is what I wish to report here for the consideration of your Highnesses, and because you will be gladdened by what I will tell you concerning Jerusalem by the same authoritative references. If there is faith, you are bound to have the victory from the enterprise.

"Your Highnesses, remember the Gospel texts and the many promises which our Savior made to us, and how all this has been put to a test: . . . The mountains will obey anyone who has faith the size of a kernel of Indian corn. All that is requested by anyone who has faith will be granted. Knock and it will be opened to you. No one should be afraid to take on any enterprise in the name of our Savior, if it is right and if the purpose is purely for his holy service . . . The working out of all things was entrusted by our Lord to each person, [but it happens] in conformity with his sovereign will, even though he gives advice to many.

"He lacks nothing that it may be in the power of men to give him. O, how good is the Lord who wishes people to perform that for which he holds himself responsible! Day and night, and at every moment, everyone should give him their most devoted thanks. . . ."[7]

THE PROVIDENTIAL HAND OF GOD IN PREPARATION FOR THE OPENING OF THE NEW WORLD

Teaching the Providential Hand of God in preparing for the opening of the New World necessitates the consideration of both the internal and external preparation that preceded and prepared the way for Columbus's voyage. These ideas of the preparation for Columbus may be covered in the previous links on the Chain of Christianity or the teacher may include these ideas in the introductory lessons for teaching the life of Columbus. See q.v. p. 34-35 for an example of reviewing and establishing the historic setting of Columbus on the Chain of Christianity.

The Bible in the Hands of the Individual

As the history of liberty is studied, the evidence is clear that the Bible in the hands of the people is causative to the establishment of Christian civil government. The door to the New World could only be opened when a people were prepared to plant on this soil a Christian form of civil government. Miss Verna Hall elucidated this truth for consideration: "Almost immediately following Wycliffe's translation of the whole Bible, God began to call forth men to develop the many scientific and economic fields which would be necessary to enable man to sail the seas, explore, and finally settle the lands across the vast Atlantic ocean. With the correlation so plain and easily documented between the Bible being made available to the individual in England, and the almost sudden development of basic inventions necessary for sailing the seas, and colonizing America, it is strange this is not better known by American Christians who have so dramatically benefitted thereby. God had been reserving the land we know as the original thirteen colonies to begin establishing the Christian form of civil government, until there could be a handful of 'peculiar people' properly rooted and grounded in His Word."[8]

Prince Henry and his School of Navigation

Prince Henry of Portugal (1394-1460), given the name "The Navigator", dedicated his life to the study of astronomy and mathematics and the encouragement of maritime expeditions for the purpose of discovering a path to India by sailing around the southern point of Africa. The fame of the Portuguese discoveries drew Christopher Columbus to Portugal, where between 1470 and 1484 he made several voyages for the Portuguese. During this period in Columbus's life, he gained the most advanced knowledge of navigation available, and became convinced that there was unknown land to the west. Once Columbus had established his plan for the westward voyage, he presented it to the Portuguese crown, suggesting that his explorations be completed under the flag of Portugal. When his plan was rejected, he appealed to the Spanish court, resolved to persevere until he found a patron who would share his ideas.

Preparation of the Man— Christopher Columbus

Columbus was inspired by the Holy Spirit to sail to the Indies, as declared in his *Book of Prophecies* (q.v. p. 10). His writings acknowledge his dependence upon the Lord to direct him. He identified his preparation in the many fields of navigation demanded by the voyage. A study of his *Journal* reveals the necessity of his being directed by the Lord as he forged the path through the unknown ocean — many biographers indicate Columbus had a "sixth sense" guiding his decisions.

THE PROVIDENTIAL PRESERVATION OF THE MAINLAND OF NORTH AMERICA UNTIL HE HAD A PEOPLE PREPARED TO ESTABLISH THE FULLEST EXPRESSION OF A CHRISTIAN CIVILIZATION

As the individual contemplates a study of Christopher Columbus from a Providential viewpoint, several questions arise which deserve consideration: Why were no efforts made for discovery of the lands to the west and establishment of permanent settlements until the late 15th century? Why, as Columbus was led by the Holy Spirit, was he drawn to the southern continent rather than the mainland of North America?

These questions were addressed by Rev. Foljambe in his sermon of 1876, "The Hand of God in American History," as he identified God's wise and beneficent timing of events as related to the discovery and preparation of America. "The discovery and preparation of this country to be the home of a great people,—the theatre of a new experiment in government, and the scene of an advancing Christian civilization,—is illustrative of this truth. Whatever may have been its prehistoric condition, for centuries it was concealed behind the mighty veil of waters from the eyes of the world. Not until the early part of the tenth century was it discovered by the Scandinavians, and only then to be hidden away again till the time should be ripe for its settlement, by a people providentially prepared for its occupancy. What a land it was, so magnificent in extent, so varied in soil and climate, so unlimited in mineral wealth and vegetable bounties; while its conformation was such as to preclude its occupants from ever being other than an united people. Harbors, and rivers, and mountain ranges link as with iron bands the far separated localities. Yet all this thorough preparation by which this continent had been builded and furnished, was not available until God's hour had come for its occupancy . . . When he had created a stalwart race, and ordained them for the settlement of his country, and for laying the foundations of a higher civilization than the world had yet seen, and when they had started on their mission of light, and freedom, and religion, then he suddenly dropped the veil from this continent, and there arose before the astonished vision of the nations the splendors of the Western World."[9]

12

PART III

TEACHER PREPARATION

Fernãd° rex hyſpania

De Inſulis inuentis

Epiſtola Criſtoſeri Colom (cui etas noſtra multũ debet : de Inſulis in mari Indico nup inuẽtis. Ad quas perquirendas octauo antea menſe:auſpicijs et ere Inuictiſſimi Fernandi Hiſoaniarum Regis miſſus fuerat) ad Magnificum dñm Raphaelez Sanxis:eiuſdẽ ſereniſſimi Regis Theſaurariũ miſſa. quam nobilis ac litterat° vir Aliander ð Coſcoi ab Hiſpano ydeomate in latinũ conuertit:tercio k̃s Maij. M.cccc.xciij. Pontificatus Alexandri Sexti Anno Primo.

Dloniam ſuſcepte prouintie rem pfectam me pſecutum fuiſſe:gratũ tibi fore ſcio:has pſhtui exarare:que te vniuſcuiuſq; rei in hoc noſtro itinere geſte inuentecq; admoneãt. Triceſimot ertio die poſtq̃ Gadibus diſceſſi:in mare Indicũ perueni:vbi plurimas Inſulas innumeris habitatas hominib° reperi:quar̃ oĩm p feliciſſimo Rege noſtro:preconio celebrato z veriſq; extenſis:cõtradicente nemine poſſeſſioné accepi primeq; earum:diui Saluatoris nomẽ impoſui (cuius fret° aurilio) tam ad hãc q̃ ad ceteras alias puenim°. Eam vero Indi

KING FERDINAND.   A FACSIMILE OF THE FIRST PAGE.

"The curious woodcuts . . . are supposed by some to have been copied from drawings made originally by Columbus himself. They give remarkable representations of the Admiral's own caravel, of his first landing on Hayti and meeting with the natives, and of the different lands that he visited." Martin's World's Fair Album-Atlas and Family Souvenir, C. Ropp and Sons, Chicago, 1892.

TO _____

This book has many joys for you;
Pictures in red and brown and blue;
Clear maps which show the sunlit seas
That hid such wondrous mysteries;
But best of all! you here will read
Of great Columbus' daring deed,
And find how wise he was and bold
Who dreamt of fair, strange lands of gold,
Sought the far borders of the main,
And gave new worlds to mighty Spain.

- Gladys M. Imlach
The Story of Columbus
E. P. Dutton & Co.

PILGRIM INSTITUTE

TEACHER PREPARATION

As the American Christian educator considers the teaching of any event or individual, the key is to determine the *Leading Ideas* to be presented to the students. The classroom content should be centered around the Idea to be taught, and supported by the facts and material selected for classroom use. The Ideas chosen must support the general Course Objectives. The following suggested general Course Objectives are reasoned from a Providential interpretation of history:

COURSE OBJECTIVES[10]

1. To recognize the Providential Hand of God in all events, past, present, and future.

2. To recognize the importance of each individual in God's plan of history.

3. To teach the major links on the Chain of Christianity.

4. To teach the Biblical principles of government which formed the American Christian Constitutional Republic, i.e., God's Principle of Individuality, The Christian Principle of Self-Government, etc.[11]

5. To learn to reason from cause to effect in historic events.

6. To recognize the stewardship responsibility of the American Christian for this nation.

DEVELOPING A GENERAL COURSE OVERVIEW

To direct the planning of the elementary history course, the teacher should prepare an overview for the year to determine the number of days or weeks to be spent on each of the nine links and its expansion. The length of time spent on each link will vary within the year, and from year to year. For example, one might spend one or two weeks on most links but six to eight weeks on just one. When a biography is to be included in the course of study, it will be necessary to include a longer period of time for the study of that particular link. In the school setting, the individual teacher should develop his Course Overview in accordance with the guidelines given by the Headmaster.

Following are suggested Course Overviews based upon the ideas identified at the First and Second Years for "Teaching America's Christian History in the Elementary School," as published in *A Guide to American Christian Education for the Home and School*, pages 201-225. The Principle Approach builds upon the concept of expanding principles and ideas. The teacher in the primary grades will build the foundation on which the understanding of America's Christian history will be deepened and expanded throughout the school curriculum. Each year's Overview includes a biography: Year One — *Columbus*, by Ingri and Edgar Parin d'Aulaire; Year Two — *Meet Christopher Columbus*, by James T. de Kay.

Each teacher must individualize his Overview to reflect the peculiar needs and background of the students being taught, adjusting appropriately for the emphases of that year's curriculum.

SUGGESTED COURSE OVERVIEW FOR YEAR ONE

I. Introduction — 1-2 weeks

    A. Definitions - history, Providence, government, self-government
    B. Individual student's history - picture, birthday, thoughts from the first day of school

II. Creation — 1-2 weeks

    A. Christian individuality
    B. The story of creation
        1. God's character
        2. God's Providence

III. Moses and the Law — 1-2 weeks

    A. Providence - as a baby
    B. Providence - in escaping Egypt
    C. Providence - in giving the Law

IV. Christ - Focal Point of History — 1-2 weeks

    A. Providence - Herod's plot to kill Christ as a baby was overthrown.
    B. All history before Christ points to His birth.
    C. Christ's coming changed history.

V. Paul and the Westward Movement of Christianity — 1-2 weeks

    A. Providence - Christ changed Paul's life.
    B. Paul's ministry from Asia to Europe moved the Chain of Christianity westward.

VI. Bible in English — 1-2 weeks

    A. Providence - God led John Wycliffe to translate the Bible into English.
    B. The Word of God brings internal liberty.

(Course Overview Continued)

VII. Christopher Columbus - Link to the New World   6-7 weeks

    A. Columbus's life forwarded the Chain of Christianity to the New World.
    B. Biography, *Columbus*, by Ingri and Edgar Parin d'Aulaire

VIII. Pilgrim - Seed of our Christian Republic   2-3 weeks

    A. The Pilgrim Story
       1. God's Providence
       2. America's heritage of Christian character
       3. First colony to establish self-government
    B. Squanto - Providential friend to the Pilgrims

IX. Patriot - First Christian Republic   5-6 weeks

    A. God's Providence in the Revolution and Constitution
    B. Biography, *George Washington*, by Ingri and Edgar Parin d'Aulaire

X. Pioneer - Westward Movement and Falling Away   7-9 weeks

    A. The Chain of Christianity moved west with the pioneers.
    B. Biography, *Abraham Lincoln*, by Ingri and Edgar Parin d'Aulaire
    C. Advancement in transportation united the nation from coast to coast.

SUGGESTED COURSE OVERVIEW FOR YEAR TWO

I. Introduction   2-3 weeks

    A. Why do we study history?
    B. Definitions — history, government, self-government
    C. God's hand of care — Providence
       1. Definition
       2. Biblical and historic examples
    D. The Chain of Christianity

II. Creation   1-2 weeks

    A. Man is God's property.
    B. Geographic individuals

(Course Overview Continued)

III. Moses and the Law   1-2 weeks

    A. God's Providence in preparing Moses to be the deliverer and lawgiver
    B. Moses, as first historian, recorded God's Providence and character from Creation through the return of the Israelites to the Promised Land.

IV. Christ - Focal Point of History   ½-1 week

    A. Christ came to change the hearts of men.
    B. Christ made internal, Christian self-government possible.

V. Paul and the Westward Movement of Christianity   ½-1 week

    A. Providence - Macedonian call
    B. Westward movement of Christianity to Europe

VI. Bible in English   2-4 weeks

    A. John Wycliffe, Morning Star of the Reformation
    B. William Tyndale, Father of the English Bible

VII. Christopher Columbus - Link to the New World   6-7 weeks

    A. God's Providence in opening the New World for exploration
    B. Biography, *Meet Christopher Columbus*, by James T. de Kay

VIII. Pilgrim - Seed of our Christian Republic   2-3 weeks

    A. The Jamestown Colony prepared the way for the Pilgrims to come to America. (Optional: Biography, *Pocahontas*, by d'Aulaire)
    B. God's Providence in the Pilgrim Story
    C. America's Heritage of Christian Character — Brotherly love and Christian care

IX. Patriot - First Christian Republic   4-5 weeks

    A. The world's first Christian Republic established upon Biblical principles of self and civil government
    B. George Washington, Father of Our Country
    C. Men of character and courage expanded the republic on the frontier — Daniel Boone.

(Course Overview Continued)

X. Pioneer - Westward Movement   7-9 weeks

    A. The obstacles to maintaining a nation of unity with diversity required Biblical character and reasoning.
    B. Biography, *Meet Abraham Lincoln*, by Barbara Cary
    C. Communication united the nation and advanced inventions and industry.
    D. Diversity with unity is demonstrated in the individuality and sovereignty of each state.

EXPANDING THE COURSE OVERVIEW

After the teacher has determined the general topics to be covered during the year, i.e., the General Course Overview, he should expand the Overview to include the specific ideas to be covered with the students. The extent of research and documentation by the teacher will be governed by the length of time appropriated for the topic in the Course Overview. The teacher's research will identify the specific facts documenting the Idea(s) which are to be presented to the students, the material to be used in the classroom, and the approach for developing the Lesson Plan. In Parts IV and V of this *Teaching Guide*, suggested Leading Ideas for each section of the two biographies have been included for consideration. The teacher should select the particular Ideas to be emphasized with the students or develop his own Ideas.

The Expanded Course Overview will be more specific as to the number of days for covering each section of the book and scheduling of projects, maps, written work, and tests. The following Expanded Course Overviews give a suggested schedule for teaching the two biographies: Year One — *Columbus*, by Ingri and Edgar Parin d'Aulaire; Year Two — *Meet Christopher Columbus*, by James T. de Kay.

CHRISTOPHER COLUMBUS - LINK TO THE NEW WORLD

DETAILED OVERVIEW

COLUMBUS
by Ingri and Edgar Parin d'Aulaire

Time allowed: 6-7 weeks

I. Introduction: Columbus on the Chain of Christianity   2-3 days

  A. Review leading ideas for the first five links. (q.v. p. 34-35)
  B. Introduce Columbus and the geographic setting of his life.

II. Columbus's childhood prepared him to fulfill God's plan. (pages 4-9)   3-4 days

  A. Individuality of Columbus
  B. Providential preparation

III. God's plan for Columbus unfolded. (pages 10-17)   5-7 days

  A. Success as a sailor prepared Columbus to be a leader.
  B. Columbus was Providentially led to new ideas and a new land.

IV. "All great and honorable actions are accompanied with great difficulties,   3-5 days
and must be both enterprised and overcome with answerable courages."*
(pages 18-23)

  - Columbus worked and waited for years to find a patron willing to help make
    his voyages possible.

V. The path to the New World was made plain through the vision, courage,   10-14 days
and steadfastness of Columbus. (pages 24-43)

  A. Columbus's belief in Divine Providence enabled him to find strength
    for himself and his crew.
  B. Hopes and dreams were fulfilled upon their arrival on the islands.
  C. Columbus was rewarded for his enterprise, faithfulness, and honor.

---

*   William Bradford, "Of Plymouth Plantation," *The Christian History of the Constitution of the United States of America,* Verna M. Hall, Compiler, (San Francisco: Foundation for American Christian Education, 1966), pp. 193-194.

(Detailed Overview Continued)

VI. "Man Proposes, God Disposes" (pages 44-57)   7-10 days

    A. Columbus had many plans—he was Providentially prevented from accomplishing some of the plans and Providentially led to accomplish far more than his highest hopes and dreams.

    B. As a leader, Columbus had to make difficult decisions, and where a weaker man might have given up, Columbus's inner strength upheld him.

    C. The character qualities of the great explorer provide an example to be followed—love of learning, imagination, perseverance, faith and steadfastness, courage, and respect for others.

    D. Christopher Columbus is a prominent discoverer to remember as the first to sail across the Atlantic and link the Old World to the New World. Many others sailed across the Atlantic Ocean because he showed the way.

CHRISTOPHER COLUMBUS - LINK TO THE NEW WORLD

DETAILED OVERVIEW

MEET CHRISTOPHER COLUMBUS
by James T. de Kay

Time allowed: 6-7 weeks

I. Introduction   2-3 days

    A. Review the Chain of Christianity.

    B. In accordance with God's timetable, He raised up an individual to lead the way to the Western hemisphere for the advancement of the gospel and its outworkings in the New World. (Chapter 1)

II. Historic and Geographic Setting (Chapter 2)   2-3 days

    A. Genoa influenced Columbus and prepared him for his future calling.

    B. Columbus's childhood and youth prepared him for great responsibilities.

(Detailed Overview Continued)

III. Providential Preservation and Placement (Chapter 3)   2-3 days

    A. Columbus's first voyage into the Western Ocean brought him to the heart of navigational activities in Portugal.
    B. The geographic setting of Columbus's life was expanded to new horizons.

IV. The Manhood of Columbus (Chapters 4 - 6)   6-8 days

    A. Columbus was Providentially directed to the individuals best suited to promote his cause.
    B. Columbus's plans for exploration gained credibility because of his own character.
    C. Queen Isabella was the lady of inspiration and vision whose ideals matched the cause of Columbus and brought her to become his patron.

V. Christopher Columbus's Great Adventure (Chapters 8 - 11)   8-9 days

    A. The European philosophy of government determined the methods Columbus used in undertaking the enterprise.
    B. God's Providence granted Columbus internal strength of character as a leader to sustain the men throughout the voyage.
    C. All of man's enterprise rests upon an understanding of the fixed principles with which the sovereign God created the universe.

VI. God's Providence Evident During Difficult Days (Chapters 12 - 16)   8-9 days

    A. The vision for which Columbus had labored during years of opposition and discouragement was at last achieved.
    B. The success of any enterprise rests upon the character of the individuals involved.
    C. Divine Providence and an increased degree of wisdom were necessary during the days of exploration and the return voyage.

VII. "To Castile and Leon Columbus gave a New World."* (Chapters 17 - 19)   4-6 days

    A. The degree of difficulty barring one's path to success is directly related to the height of honor when the enterprise is accomplished.
    B. "Western Europe received all the wisdom and experience of the ancient world . . . and her children, rich in her experience, instructed at once by her success and her mistakes and aided always by her wisdom, found (let us hope) in America the goal of their noblest aspirations."§

*   Washington Irving, *The Life and Voyages of Christopher Columbus,* (Chicago: Hooper, Clarke, & Co.).
§   Charles Bancroft, "The Footprints of Time," *The Christian History of the Constitution of the United States of America,* Verna M. Hall, Compiler, (San Francisco: Foundation for American Christian Education, 1966), p. 8.

As the teacher researches the material for classroom use, it is necessary to guide this research to discern the key Ideas to be considered for teaching the students. Miss Katherine Dang has identified four approaches for the teacher to use in research and lesson preparation, including the study of *Key Individuals, Key Events, Key Institutions,* and *Key Documents*. The material researched is organized on charts which are used in the teacher's planning. Refer to *A Guide to American Christian Education for the Home and School*, pages 308-322, for assistance in planning and organizing the material to be covered in the classroom.

DEVELOPING LESSON PLANS

Upon the completion of adequate research, the teacher is prepared to develop the specific plans for daily instruction. To provide a classroom which will produce a love of learning in the student, a variety of approaches to the daily classtime should be included in the plans—consideration must always be given to the age and capacity of the students. Kindergarten students will enjoy listening to the story as it is read aloud, looking at the illustrations, discussing the ideas, outlining simple maps, and coloring simple pictures. Primary age students may read the book aloud together during the classtime, reason concerning the main ideas, record simple notes, answer written questions, outline maps, and color pictures. Students of all ages enjoy special projects and events which enhance the material and bring it to life.

The Idea to be comprehended by the student must be clearly identified by the teacher and must govern the content of the classtime and any student work. Suggested Ideas have been given for teaching Christopher Columbus.

CLASSTIME

Many options are available for the teacher to consider in the teaching of Christopher Columbus:
● The teacher may produce handouts for the primary student to read. Some original resource material, appropriate for the ability of the students, may be included. Students enjoy the opportunity of underlining, highlighting, or developing marginal notes as they reason from the material presented.
● Specific direction has been included in this *Teaching Guide* for two biographies of Columbus — *Columbus* by Ingri and Edgar Parin d'Aulaire, and *Meet Christopher Columbus* by James T. de Kay. If taught to kindergarten students, the d'Aulaire biography should be read aloud by the teacher. Primary age students will enjoy reading either biography aloud during class. Students of all ages can be challenged to draw conclusions related to the Idea being considered for the day. A variety of questions have been included, from which the teacher may guide the classroom reasoning or appropriate student written work.
● Maps are invaluable for the student's understanding of not only where the events occurred, but to see the Hand of God in the veiling of the North American continent.
● Students always enjoy dramatizing a key event of history. Many opportunities are afforded in the life of Christopher Columbus, i.e., Columbus's arrival in Portugal, his petition to King Ferdinand and Queen Isabella, the near mutiny of the sailors and final sighting of land, etc. These plays may be kept as simple or as complex as desired by the teacher. Spontaneity and more elaborate projects are both enjoyed by the students.

STUDENT RECORDING

It is essential that, by the first grade, the main Ideas to be remembered by the student become a part of their permanent record in the notebook, with adequate facts to support the Idea. When reading a biography, the teacher is not compelled to record material from each chapter, but should consider the Ideas which are to remain with the student. This recording may be accomplished in a variety of ways:

- Charts showing contrasts, comparisons, cause to effect, or effect to cause are effective in developing reasoning skills.
- A timeline demonstrates the Providence of God in events of history.
- Simplified charts identifying *Key Events, Key Individuals, Key Institutions,* and *Key Documents* may be used in teaching and recording leading ideas and facts.
- Outlines may be utilized by the teacher, but should be complete for one day or unit of teaching, keeping the teacher and student from becoming encumbered by the tedium of the outline.

For the primary age student, the charts, timelines, or outlines are kept simple in their form and content.

STUDENT WRITTEN WORK

The confirmation of the Idea being taught will occur as the student has the opportunity to reflect and reason concerning the Idea taught and complete research and recording of his individual thoughts and conclusions. The student work should be devised to require not just the recording of facts, but demand reasoning from the Leading Idea being considered. These exercises must be evaluated as to their appropriateness for the capacity of the students and the preparation given during the classtime.

- Pictures illustrating the events studied are enjoyed by students of all ages. Original art may be checked as to its accuracy in representation of the event.
- Maps provide an excellent opportunity for the student to produce a geographical essay which confirms his comprehension of the Idea covered. See *A Guide to American Christian Education for the Home and School*, page 272, for direction in producing maps.
- Questions which involve short answers may be given. Consider that questions asking who, what, when, and where are fact-centered and identify the student's comprehension, but do not require reasoning. Questions addressing why, considering cause to effect or effect to cause, or expecting the student to draw conclusions demand the student's reasoning capacity. The teacher should keep in mind that questions which demand reasoning will require more time in answering than simply reproducing facts which have been presented.
- Short essays may be written by the primary student; a first grade student should be able to write a simple essay by the second semester. Essays should be specifically related to the Idea which the teacher has presented in the classroom.
- By second semester of first grade, simple guided research may be performed by the student, i.e. further study relative to some aspect of Columbus's life—navigational tools available to Columbus; geography of Genoa, Italy, the Canary Islands, or the West Indies; details of the ships used by Columbus; further details relating to the life of the explorer or perhaps the Indians at this historic period. For the primary student, the teacher would probably find it best to have the resources which are appropriate for the grade level available in the classroom and provide questions which would guide the student in his research.
- The student may keep a daily journal (log) of the voyage, identifying the difficult decisions which Columbus was required to make concerning the direction of the ship, the threats of mutiny by the sailors, and the many challenges of the voyage.

SAMPLE LESSON PLANS

The lesson plan is the brief notation of the material which the teacher intends to cover in a given classtime. The lesson plan enables the teacher to prepare for a class ahead of time and then to review quickly what should be taught. The lesson plan also serves as a record of the material covered and may be used for review, make-up lessons, test preparation, etc. Teachers who use lesson plan books that allow minimal space for recording information may find it helpful to prepare lesson plans and keep them in their class notebook, and transfer abbreviated plans into the actual lesson plan book.

Teachers might find it beneficial to prepare lesson plans for a complete section of their expanded overview at one time. When beginning the lesson plans for each section of the overview, the teacher could write the leading idea for each day into the lesson plan before including the specific information necessary for the class. Planning for one or two weeks at a time helps insure that the teacher will cover the amount of material necessary during that time and also allows for a continuous train of thought rather than individual, isolated lessons.

Several essentials should be included in the lesson plan: summary statement of the leading idea to be covered, reading, discussion, notes, and student written work. As stated previously, a key ingredient in preparing lessons is variety; the teacher should attempt to incorporate into the lesson plans different teaching methodologies, including various types of discussion, notes, and student work.

Following are sample lesson plans for teaching one week's lessons from each biography. They are intended for kindergarten and lower elementary classrooms, with a classtime of approximately fifteen to twenty minutes.

SAMPLE LESSON PLANS

COLUMBUS
by Ingri and Edgar Parin d'Aulaire

DAY ONE

Leading Idea: The Chain of Christianity shows God's working in the lives of men and nations.

Discussion:
1. Review definitions of history and Providence.
2. Using a visual representation of the Chain of Christianity, have students relate the leading ideas for the first three links. (q.v. p. 34-35)
3. Incorporate appropriate songs, poetry, and map review throughout the lesson.

Day Two

Leading Idea: God opened the New World for discovery at just the right time.

Discussion:
1. Using a visual Chain of Christianity, have the students relate the leading ideas for the next two links. (q.v. p. 35)
2. Introduce Christopher Columbus as the link to the New World. (q.v. p. 35)

Day Three

Leading Idea: God created Columbus with the unique interests, spirit, and abilities to be a sailor.

Read:
Columbus, pages 4-5

Discussion:
1. Recite the poem, "God Made Me Special." How did God make Columbus special?
2. Find Genoa, Italy on a map. If God wanted Columbus to be a sailor, why was Genoa an excellent place for him to live?

Student Activity:
1. Study the picture. Compare Christopher's toy boat with the shuttle his father used for weaving.
2. Make a toy boat.

Day Four

Leading Idea: The busy activities of a seaport intrigued Columbus and planted within him the desire to visit faraway places.

Read:
Columbus, pages 6-7

Discussion:
1. Look at a map or globe. How did sailors travel between Italy and Asia?
2. Study the picture. What is in Christopher's hand? What might he have been thinking about?
3. Did Columbus learn about the world only in school? How else did he learn?

Student Activity:
Take the students on a walk. Upon returning, allow each student to relate what he learned by observation.

DAY FIVE

Leading Idea: Christopher admired the beauty of God's creation and desired to learn all he could about the earth.

Read:
Columbus, page 8

Discussion:
1. Study the picture and discuss the individuality of China.
2. What did the other boys admire about Christopher?
3. How did Columbus help his father? How did that help him learn useful lessons?

Student Activity:
Using an orange, make a model of the earth similar to the picture on page 8.

The lesson plans given above are fairly detailed. However, they could be summarized in a lesson plan book as identified below:

Day One	Day Two	Day Three	Day Four	Day Five
LI: Chain of Chr.	LI: Provid. Timing	LI: Individuality of Columbus Read: *Columbus* pp.4-5	LI: Columbus wanted to sail Read: *Columbus* pp. 6-7	LI: Christopher wanted to learn Read: *Columbus* p. 8

Disc: Review -
- Def.-hist./Prov.
- Chain of Chr.
  (Creation to Christ)
	Disc: - Review Chain
	  of Chr. (Paul-Bible)
	- Intro. Columbus
	  on Chain of Chr.
		Disc: Recite "God Made
		  Me Special"
		- Columbus's Ind.
		- Genoa/Providence
		  (Provid. place)
		- Toy boat/shuttle
			Disc: - Travel from Italy
			  to Asia
			- Compare orange to
			  globe
			- How did Columbus
			  learn?
				Disc: - Individ. of China
				- Christopher's abilities
				- Columbus helped/
				  learned

SA: —	SA: —	SA: Make a toy boat	SA: Walk/Relate observ.	SA: Make model with orange

LI = Leading Idea   Disc = Discussion   SA = Student Activity

SAMPLE LESSON PLANS

MEET CHRISTOPHER COLUMBUS
by James T. de Kay

DAY ONE

Leading Idea: Review the contribution of each link on Chain of Christianity

Discussion:
Have students review the Chain of Christianity, from Creation to the Bible in English.
1. Review definitions of history, Providence, government, and self-government.
2. Creation
    -Man is God's property.
    -Geographic individuals
3. Moses
    -Preparation to be deliverer and lawgiver
    -Contribution as first historian
4. Christ - internal self-government made possible
5. Paul - Westward movement of Christianity to Europe
6. Bible in English - The Word of God brought liberty in preparation for the Westward movement to the New World.

DAY TWO

Leading Idea: In accordance with God's timetable, He raised up a man to lead the way to the Western hemisphere for the advancement of the gospel and its outworkings in the New World.

Read:
Meet Christopher Columbus, Chapter 1. Optional reading for students or teacher: Selection from *Meet Christopher Columbus,* 1968 edition, q.v. p. 57.

Discussion:
1. God gave Columbus a special dream. What was it?
2. How was Columbus's attitude about the Western Ocean different from others of his time?
3. Compare an actual globe to the way Columbus believed the world to be.

Student Work:
1. In order to be a leader, a person must have goals and dreams. What dream did Columbus have?
2. To accomplish his goals, Columbus needed certain character qualities. What were they?

DAY THREE

Leading Ideas: Columbus grew up in the Providential revival of geographic interest.
The setting in which an individual lives is an influence on his life, but his choices determine
its course.

Read:
Meet Christopher Columbus, Chapter 2, pages 8-9

Discussion:
1. How did Genoa influence Columbus's chosen occupation and prepare him to fulfill it?
2. Who arranged his life so that these influences could be in place?
3. How is sailing controlled by the weather?

Class Activity:
Begin working on a map of Italy showing the geographic setting of Columbus's boyhood.

DAY FOUR

Leading Idea: Navigation was a rigorous school and the sea a demanding schoolmaster, causing
Columbus to be a responsible youth.

Read:
Meet Christopher Columbus, Chapter 2, pages 9-10

Discussion:
1. Study pictures of sailing and discuss with the students the methods and instruments sailors used to navigate the seas. Reason with the students to discern the differences between sailing and traveling on land.
2. Identify the ingredients of a good sailor.

Class Activities:
1. Prepare a large diagram of a ship and have the students locate various parts of the ship mentioned on page 9. Also, see pages 30-31.
2. Sing enjoyable songs about sailing.

Student Work:
Continue the map work. Include specific locations noted in Chapter 2.

DAY FIVE

Leading Idea: Sailing required skill and a love of adventure.

Class Activity:
Visit a museum or prepare a special activity centered around the art of rope making, sailing, etc.

Student Work:
Write a sentence describing an activity Christopher Columbus would have done on his voyages.

Day One	Day Two	Day Three	Day Four	Day Five
LI: Chain of Chr.	LI: Provid. Timing	LI: - Geographic Interest/ Influence on Columbus	LI: Columbus learns from sailing	LI: Sailing-skill/ adventure
	Read: *Meet Col.*, Ch. 1	Read: *Meet Col.*, Ch. 2, pp. 8-9	Read: *Meet Col.*, pp. 9-10	
Disc: Review-Def.-history, Providence, gov't, self-gov't - Creation-Bible in Eng.	Disc: - Columbus's dream - Columbus unafraid of Ocean - Comp. globe/Col. ideas	Disc: - Genoa's influence - Providence - Sailing/Weather	Disc: Pictures - Compare sailing/travel - Diagram of ship - Qualities of sailor	
CA: —	CA: —	CA: Map of Italy	CA: Sing songs - sailing	CA: Visit museum/activity about sailing
SA: —	SA: Questions	SA: —	SA: Map - label/outline	SA: Describe activity of Columbus as sailor (1 sent.)

LI = Leading Ideas   Disc = Discussion   CA = Class Activities   SA = Student Activities

PART IV

COLUMBUS

by Ingri and Edgar Parin d'Aulaire

A DREAM OF CATHAY.
*(Every boy of spirit in those days of adventure felt certain that he could
find and conquer that land of fable.)*

SAILING TO DISTANT LANDS.

The True Story of Christopher Columbus
by Elbridge S. Brooks
D. Lothrop Company, ©1892

━━ PILGRIM INSTITUTE ━━

Section I

COLUMBUS
by Ingri and Edgar Parin d'Aulaire

Introduction

". . . America adopts the children of all lands only to return a manhood ennobled by a sense of its own dignity through the practice of a system of self-government which improves the condition and promotes the interest of each while it produces harm to none.

"America, made up of individuals from all nations and continents, and belonging to all races, does indeed adopt many children, who, in turn, enrich America by their contributions of character and talent.

"The d'Aulaires, a talented husband-and-wife team, both write and illustrate books for younger children. Ingri was born and educated in Norway. Edgar came from Switzerland where his father was famous as a portrait painter. They met in Paris, both students of art, and eventually they came to America. They decided, like so many millions of other individuals, that America should become home for them. Anne Carroll Moore, a well-known Children's Librarian, suggested that they combine their talents and produce beautiful books for children—so they began. . . .

"While working on their book *Columbus* the d'Aulaires spent two years collecting materials and visiting every spot which they describe and illustrate. This included trips to the Old World—to Italy and to Spain, gathering their historical and artistic data. They sketched, visited, and made notes on the spot. Then they traveled back to the New World

locations in the Caribbean. Here they sailed to the actual islands discovered by Columbus and met some of the last descendants of those Carib Indians with whom Columbus had so many dealings."[12]

Miss Rosalie Slater has highlighted the work of the d'Aulaires in her *Family Program for Reading Aloud*. Pages 25-29 provide inspirational and instructional assistance in the unique form of art the d'Aulaires implemented as well as principles and leading ideas for teaching Christopher Columbus on the Chain of Christianity.

The biography, *Columbus*, by Ingri and Edgar Parin d'Aulaire, is a beautifully written and illustrated text for reading aloud to young children. Their attention will be captured and their imagination sparked by the large, detailed illustrations which so perfectly complement the written text. The book lends itself easily into divisions of one to two pages per lesson.

Following are ideas, questions, and activities to guide the teacher in preparing lessons which promote observation, reflection, and reasoning. The suggested discussion, student work, and activities have been designed for kindergarten students who are still mastering the skills of reading and writing. If the book is taught to older students, additional written work could be required.

HISTORIC AND GEOGRAPHIC SETTING

History is the beautiful record of God's working in the lives of men and nations to accomplish His Divine purposes. The course provides opportunity for teachers and students alike to recognize the Hand of God, the character and blessings of liberty, and ideas and principles necessary for liberty to be perpetuated. Nine expanding links on the Chain of Christianity have been recommended for the elementary history curriculum. (q.v. p. 5) As the Columbus biography is introduced to the student, each of the links previously taught should be reviewed, with its leading ideas, for the student to grasp each stepping-stone in the development of individual and civil liberty.

LEADING IDEAS

CREATION

God is in control of all history.

• Review the beginning of history — Genesis 1:1.

Only God is able to make everything—the earth, sun, moon, stars, plants, animals and people—out of nothing. He is a mighty and powerful God.

Sing appropriate songs or recite poetry highlighting God as Creator. These should be review from earlier teaching in the year: "All Things Bright and Beautiful," "I Sing the Mighty Power of God," etc.

• Review *God's Principle of Individuality.*[13]

Everything that God made is very special. Are any two snowflakes exactly alike? Are any two leaves exactly alike? Are any two people exactly alike?

God made each individual in a very special way. Recite the poem, "God Made Me Special,"[14] or other poems, songs, or verses which the students may have already learned.

• Review geographic individuality of the continents.

Call on students to name each of the four continents in the Eastern hemisphere. Which continent is the largest? Which is the smallest? Which three are the closest together?

Why did these continents have the most people living on them? What would be the easiest way to travel from Asia to Europe? From Asia to Africa? From Europe to Africa? Students might be allowed to go to the map, point out the various continents, and trace the route from one continent to another.

MOSES

God's preservation of Moses to fulfill His plan.

• On which continent is the land God promised to the Israelites? Where were the Israelites living when Moses was born? What wicked law did the Pharaoh have?

• How did God protect Moses? Who was sent by God to find Moses? Why was she the very best person to find him?

God's preparation of Moses to lead the Israelites.

• When Moses grew up to be a man, he led the Israelites back to their country. What special miracles did God perform while they

34

travelled? Review appropriate songs highlighting the Providence of God in Israel's escape from Egypt—"How did Moses Cross the Red Sea?", etc.

CHRIST

> ### *God's fulfillment of prophecies.*

● Where did God promise that His Son would be born? Mary and Joseph did not live there, so how did God cause them to leave their home and go to exactly the right place?

> ### *Christ, the focal point of history.*

● How did God tell the shepherds and wise men that His Son was born? His birth was the most important birth of all history. He came and died so that men and nations could have liberty.

> ### *God's Providential protection of His Son.*

● The shepherds and wise men loved Him, but the king did not. How did God protect baby Jesus from the king?

> ### *God's provision of a Saviour for man.*

● Why did God send His Son to the world? How did Christ's coming provide the opportunity for Christian self-government?

● Review key verses the students have learned which identify the purpose of Christ's coming, i.e., John 3:16, Luke 19:10, etc.

PAUL

> ### *The movement of Christianity westward.*

● People in Asia heard about Jesus because Jesus and His disciples lived there. How did people in Europe hear about Jesus?

● How did God direct Paul to Europe?

● Find Greece on a map of Europe. How did Paul travel from Asia to Greece?

BIBLE IN ENGLISH

> ### *God provided the man to translate the Bible into English so that all could read it.*

● Hundreds of years after Paul, the people in Europe knew about Jesus, but why couldn't they read the Bible?

● Where did John Wycliffe live? How much did he love God's Word? How much did he love the people of his country? How did God use him to help England?

CHRISTOPHER COLUMBUS

> ### *Link to the New World*

● Many times in history God has used people to discover new and exciting things about His creation. Five hundred years ago, a man who was always interested in learning about new places, new people, and new things had a great adventure. He was one of the first men with enough courage to sail across the ocean, and God used him to find an important surprise.

● Find Greece on a map of Europe. Just west of Greece is another special and interesting country. What shape does Italy have?

● Have several students practice going to a large map or globe and finding Italy. Point out the Americas and identify briefly how God used Columbus in their discovery.

BULLETIN BOARD SUGGESTION

It is essential to the study of History that students understand the relationship between events, individuals, and God's Providence in the advancement of the Gospel. Teachers may wish to prepare a wall display for the classroom reflecting the Chain of Christianity's westward movement, which can be used for teaching and frequent review. Suggestion: Place a timeline above the chalkboard, including all the links of the Chain of Christianity which are to be taught that year. Pictures representing each of the links may be joined together on a timeline or by a small chain. This will prove an excellent tool for teaching in other classes, as the teacher can identify the historic setting for the life of a specific author, scientist, mathematician, etc.

Section II

COLUMBUS'S CHILDHOOD PREPARED HIM TO FULFILL GOD'S PLAN

CONCERNING THE BIRTHPLACE, FAMILY, AND NAME OF THE ADMIRAL CHRISTOPHER COLUMBUS

"Two things which are important to know about every famous man are his birthplace and family, because men generally accord more honor to those who were born in great cities and of noble parents. Therefore some wished me to tell how the Admiral came of illustrious stock, although misfortune had reduced his parents to great poverty and need . . .

"But I have spared myself such labor, believing that the Admiral was chosen for his great work by Our Lord, who desired him as His true Apostle to follow the example of others of His elect by publishing His name on distant seas and shores, not in cities and palaces, thereby imitating Our Lord himself, who though his descent was from the blood royal of Jerusalem, yet was content to have his parentage from an obscure source. Similarly, the Admiral, although endowed with all the qualities that his great task required, chose to leave in obscurity all that related to his birthplace and family . . .

"Reflecting on this, I was moved to believe that just as most of his affairs were directed by a secret Providence, so the variety of his name and surname was not without its mystery . . ."[15]

● Washington Irving's biography of Christopher Columbus provides a fine resource for the teacher's further understanding of the life and work of Columbus. Selected sections of Irving's work have been included for the teacher's consideration, q.v. p. 79.

LEADING IDEAS

When presenting each day's lesson, the teacher should have specific goals. The main goal should be to teach a leading idea through the reading, facts, discussion, and other class activities. *This leading idea is a conclusion to which the teacher should reason with the students.*

Leading ideas from the text are highlighted in boxes, with supporting ideas following. Each teacher must determine the leading ideas to be emphasized with the students. Although numerous ideas have been identified, the teacher should not endeavor to be comprehensive of all these ideas, but must consider the age and capacity of the students.

INDIVIDUALITY OF CHRISTOPHER COLUMBUS
Pages 4-5

> *God created Columbus with the unique interests, spirit, and abilities to be a sailor.*

● Recite the poem, "God Made me Special." How did God make Columbus special?

● Note the location of Genoa on a map of Italy. If God wanted Columbus to be a sailor, why was Genoa an excellent place for Columbus to live?

● The picture on page 4 of the biography notes the legend of Saint Christopher. Columbus's son commented on his name in light of this story:
". . . And if we give his name its Latin form, which is Christophorus Colonus, we may say that just as St. Christopher is reported to have gotten that name because he carried Christ over deep waters with great danger to himself, and just as he conveyed over people whom no other could have carried, so the Admiral Christophorus Colonus, asking Christ's aid and protection in that perilous pass, crossed over with his company that the Indian nations might become dwellers in the triumphant Church of Heaven."[16]

● Divine Providence enables individuals to achieve their God-given purpose on the Chain of Christianity. (*Concerning the Birthplace, Family, and Name of the Admiral Christopher Columbus*, q.v. p. 37)

PROVIDENTIAL PREPARATION FOR DISCOVERY
Pages 6-7

> *The busy activities of a seaport intrigued Columbus and planted within him the desire to visit faraway places.*

● Look at a map or globe. How did sailors travel from Asia to Italy?

● In the picture on page 7, what does Columbus have in his hand? What might he have been thinking about?

● Did Columbus learn about the world only in school? How else did he learn?

CHRISTOPHER USES HIS IMAGINATION
Pages 8-9

> *Christopher admired the beauty of God's creation and desired to learn all he could about the earth.*

● From what country is the little boy at the bottom of the picture on page 8? Look at his hair and the shape of the houses. Have one of the students find China on a map. Perhaps Mr. and Mrs. d'Aulaire chose to draw a picture of a little boy from China since Columbus wanted to sail to China.

If the students have read *The Story about Ping*, remind the children of some details about the story so that they remember the individuality of China.

● What did the other boys admire about Christopher?

● How did Columbus help his father? How did that help him to learn useful lessons?

STUDENT ACTIVITIES

A variety of projects and activities have been suggested to assist the teacher in bringing the study of Christopher Columbus to life for the students. These activities are enjoyable opportunities to increase the student's understanding of Columbus's life, the nations used Providentially to open the New World, and the character which enabled Columbus to be a leader of discovery.

● Look at the picture of Columbus and his father on page 5. What is in Columbus's hand? What is in his father's hand? The shapes are similar. If Columbus's father had had an old shuttle, how could he have made it into a toy ship?

Using poster board, wooden sticks, construction paper, and glue, help each student make a toy ship.

● Demonstrate weaving to the class. The children could do a simple weaving project with a child's loom or by using strips of paper. Visit craft shops or the library for ideas.

● Take the students on a walk, during which no one is allowed to talk or ask questions. Upon returning to the room, allow each child to tell about something they learned by just listening and looking.

● Using oranges, grapefruit, or colored styrofoam balls, have the student make a model of a butterfly creeping around a sphere. (See picture on page 9 of the biography.) A sticker or a small cut-out butterfly may be placed onto a straight pin and pushed into the orange. Students can imagine how the wings of the butterfly could seem like a ship to young Christopher.

Place butterflies on opposite sides of the orange. Would people on the other side of the world be standing on their heads?

● *Suggested Student Activities, #1, q.v. p. 107.*

Section III

GOD'S PLAN FOR COLUMBUS UNFOLDED

LEADING IDEAS

CHRISTOPHER'S FIRST SAILING ADVENTURES
Pages 10-11

> *Christopher found the great desire of his heart fulfilled on board the ships where he became well-known as a master seaman.*

● God wanted Columbus to learn to be an excellent sailor. First he sailed in a sea much smaller than the ocean so that he could become one of the very best sea captains. Using a map, compare the size of the Mediterranean Sea to the size of the Atlantic Ocean. Which is bigger, the Mediterranean Sea or the Atlantic Ocean? God was preparing Columbus to sail to faraway places.

● Why was Columbus able to be a leader? How did Columbus show great courage during this time?

● What did the sailors mean when they said, "here was a captain with bone in his nose"? Have the students feel their noses. How does it feel at the end? How does it feel at the top? Which part is the strongest?

GOD PROVIDENTIALLY PLACED COLUMBUS IN A NEW COUNTRY
Pages 12-13

> *In some of Columbus's darkest and most difficult hours, God was working to lead him to exactly the right place.*

● Find the Strait of Gibraltar on a map. Identify each of the countries near which Columbus was sailing.

● When Columbus lost his ship it was very sad, but God brought him to the best country for learning even more about sailing. Portugal had the most learning about sailing, ships, and important countries for buying valuable things.

● What is a pirate? Have students think of a Bible story in which thieves attacked a traveler. How did God care for the traveler?

● How did God protect Columbus from the pirates? How did God keep him from the pirates when he was swimming to shore?

● Columbus could have been feeling sorry for himself because he had lost his ship.

Instead, how did he feel? How did God use the pirates to help Columbus?

● Find China and India on a map. People in Europe wanted to buy spices, cloth, and other goods from China. The trip by land was too long and dangerous, so sea captains were searching for a pathway by water to the Indies.

COLUMBUS'S NEW IDEA
Pages 14-15

At just the right time, God gave Columbus the desire to sail west.

● How did Columbus show that he loved his family?

● Have students practice finding east and west on a map. Find Portugal on the map. What direction would the sailors travel to find India and China?

● Study a globe. How was Columbus's idea of sailing to India and China different from the ideas of others? What questions did he have about sailing west around the world to reach India and China? No one could answer his questions because no one had ever sailed west across the Atlantic Ocean. Which ocean is bigger—the Atlantic or the Pacific? How did Columbus learn everything he could about the Atlantic Ocean?

KNOWING HISTORY HELPED COLUMBUS
Pages 16-17

Long before Columbus was born, adventurous men such as Leif Erikson, Marco Polo, and others had set off by land and sea for unknown places. Their examples encouraged Columbus to undertake his enterprise to the Indies.

● Find Iceland, Norway, and Greenland on a map. Trace the voyage of Leif Erikson. This story helped Columbus know that he could sail west across the ocean. What kept this story from being forgotten for 500 years?

● Where did Columbus think Leif Erikson had landed? Of what continents had the people heard?

● What did Columbus believe that God wanted him to do? What did he need to have in order to do this?

● Research Norway and the story of Leif Erikson's adventures. Find pictures to show the class and, if possible, to color. The Norwegian embassy may be a good source for posters, pictures, and information.

STUDENT ACTIVITIES

● Have each student identify Italy and England on a map of Europe. Over the next several days have the students work on outlining these two countries. Other countries may be added to the map as they become a part of the story.

The map should be simple and large so that the students can use crayons to outline neatly. Have them use blue to outline the water and another color for the land. It will take several days to work on the map. Outlining is intense work and can become tedious, rather than pleasant, if the students do too much work at one time. See page 272 of *A Guide to American Christian Education* by James B. Rose for further details on map work.

• Have the students outline Portugal on the map of Europe.

• Plan a Norwegian Day Celebration. Write a letter to the parents explaining what the children have learned. Make suggestions of how the children can dress in special costumes. Recruit mothers to find or prepare special Norwegian treats for the children.

• *Suggested Student Activities, #2, q.v. p. 107.*

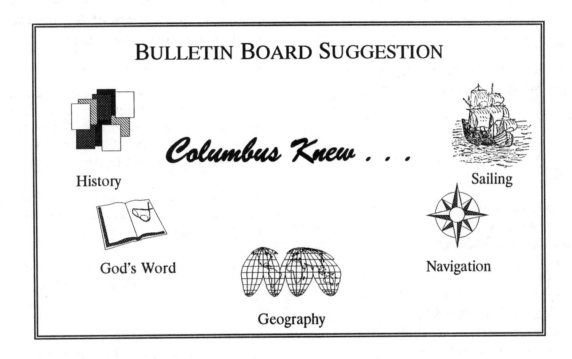

Section IV

"ALL GREAT AND HONORABLE ACTIONS ARE ACCOMPANIED WITH GREAT DIFFICULTIES, AND MUST BE BOTH ENTERPRISED AND OVERCOME WITH ANSWERABLE COURAGES"[17]

LEADING IDEAS

COLUMBUS WAITED PATIENTLY FOR HELP
Pages 18-19

Although others disapproved of his plan, Columbus did not give up.

● Why didn't the Portuguese think Columbus could sail across the ocean? Consider the picture on page 18: Why is the man laughing?

● Why did the king decide not to help Columbus? When the Portuguese decided not to help Columbus, what did he do? Students need to know that if something is important, one should not give up, no matter how difficult it is.

● Find Spain on a map. God had given Spain a good and wise Queen, who, in time,

would be a Providential tool to aid Columbus in his explorations.

● Find Africa on a map. Explain to the students how the Moors invaded Spain. Teachers may wish to research the story of El Cid and the Spanish victory over the Moors to increase their own understanding of the historic setting.

COLUMBUS WAITED AGAIN TO FIND HELP
Pages 20-21

In God's perfect time, friends were raised up to help Columbus along the path to success.

● How many years did Columbus wait for the King and Queen of Spain to help him?

45

Columbus knew his idea was good and was willing to work and wait to make his voyage.

• How was it difficult for Columbus to wait? What friends did God provide to help Columbus with his plan? What happened to encourage Columbus that the King and Queen might be ready to help him?

GOD HELPED COLUMBUS PREPARE FOR THE VOYAGE
Pages 22-23

> *Great deeds are accomplished by men and women who are willing to give up their time, their property, and sometimes even their lives.*

• Find the flag with Isabella's coat of arms in the picture. What weapons and protection did the soldiers use in fighting? When King Saul asked David to fight Goliath, he wanted David to wear his armor. Why couldn't David wear King Saul's armor?

• How did the King and Queen want to celebrate after they had won the war for their country? What sacrifices was the queen willing to make in order to help Columbus? How much would the King and Queen give Columbus if he was able to sail to the Indies?

• What provisions did the King and Queen give Columbus to make his voyage?

• When Columbus sailed in the Mediterranean Sea he had no trouble in finding men to sail with him. Why was it difficult now? What character did both Columbus and the sailors need? Consider Bible characters who had the courage to be true to their ideas, i.e. David, Daniel, Esther, Shadrach, Meshach, Abednego. When is that character quality needed?

STUDENT ACTIVITIES

• Read the poem, "In Columbus' Time," by Annette Wynne, to the students. Discuss how Columbus would eventually be shown to be wise rather than the King's "wise men." Students would enjoy reciting this poem together as a class.

• Have the students outline Spain on a map of Europe.

• *Suggested Student Activities*, #3-8, q.v. p. 107.

IN COLUMBUS' TIME

Suppose you lived then, do you think that you
Would believe what Columbus said was true,
Or would you be like the wise men who
Laughed in his face and said, "Pooh, pooh?"

- Annette Wynne
For Days and Days
J.B. Lippincott Co., 1919

Section V

THE PATH TO THE NEW WORLD WAS MADE PLAIN THROUGH THE VISION, COURAGE, AND STEADFASTNESS OF COLUMBUS

LEADING IDEAS

IMPORTANT BEGINNINGS FOR THE VOYAGE
Pages 24-25

> *Columbus led his men in prayer before beginning the voyage, helping them to recognize their dependence upon God for a safe and prosperous voyage.*

● How did Columbus show that he believed God could protect and care for them on the voyage?

● Which ship can be seen in the picture? Find the coat of arms which shows that Queen Isabella helped provide Columbus with the ships for his voyage.

● What did the men promise Columbus before they left the church? Why did they have their hands on the Bible?

● Have the students observe the river in the picture. Was the water really red? Why did the d'Aulaires color the water red?

● How did the women and children feel about the voyage? How did the church let the whole town know that the men were leaving? Today, how does news travel about what is happening in the world?

COLUMBUS HELPED HIS MEN STAY STRONG
Pages 26-27

> *When the sailors were afraid and wanted to go back, Columbus helped them overcome their fears and continue their voyage.*

● How did the sailors show that they had great courage? Why were they excited about the voyage?

- Look at the course of the voyage on a map. Locate the Canary Islands. Why did the men become frightened? Show the direction on the map which Columbus was following. How did he know which direction was west?

- What subject did Columbus need to know in order to sail the ships?

- Besides being afraid, what other problems did the sailors have?

COURAGE, CHRISTOPHER COLUMBUS
Pages 28-29

When difficulties and discouragement overcame the crew, Columbus patiently helped the men renew their courage.

- Find the crow's nest in the picture. Why did the sailors go up in the crow's nest?

- How did Columbus help his men to have courage? Who helped Columbus have courage?

- Who makes the wind? Was it any harder for God to make the wind when the ships were further away from Spain?

- Show the students a compass. Why was this their best way of finding direction?

- Why was it so frightening for the sailors when the compass was no longer accurate?

- Have students observe Columbus in the picture. Why wasn't he afraid of the seaweed?

"SAIL ON! SAIL ON! AND ON! . . ."[18]
Pages 30-31

One man, Christopher Columbus, was responsible for keeping his men on course and helping them to maintain their strong hope.

- Were the sailors happy about having the wind they needed to continue sailing? What kept the sailors from going back home?

- How did Columbus encourage his men to keep sailing? Look at the picture. When the sailors looked far ahead, what did they see? How did it trick them?

- What did the carved stick mean? What did the branch and flowers mean? What did flocks of birds mean? Why did Columbus change the direction they were sailing? How did these signs encourage the sailors?

LAND AT LAST
Pages 32-33

After long weeks of sailing, land was sighted at last, and God allowed the crew to arrive safely.

- The sailors were anxious and excited to find land. What were the men doing? What is the sailor in the crow's nest using so that he can see farther than anyone else?

- The night that Columbus noticed a different type of light, there may have been others looking for land also. Why did he notice it when others did not?

● Explain what a reef is. Look back at the picture on page 29. Find the anchor. Show how the anchor needed to stay up in order for the ship to sail, but could hold the ship in place when dropped into the water.

CLAIMING THE LAND
Pages 34-35

> *All were happy to have arrived on the beautiful shore where Columbus thanked the Lord for their safe voyage and claimed the land for Spain.*

● How did the land seem extremely good to the sailors after their long voyage, storms at sea, and stale food?

● Study the picture and locate the following: each of the ships, Queen Isabella's flag, some new animals Columbus had never seen before, the sailors, and some Indians.

● What was the last thing Columbus did before leaving Spain? What was the first thing Columbus did when he arrived on land?

● Find China and India on a map. Columbus did not know there were two continents in the Atlantic Ocean between Europe and Asia. How did he know the people were not Chinese? Why did he think they were Indians?

● What had Columbus and the sailors expected to find when they landed? What did they find instead?

● Use a map to locate the island Columbus named San Salvador. (q.v. p. 109) Columbus named the island in honor of Jesus because He is the Savior. Ask the students to think of a Bible word that begins like "Salvador"?

THE WEALTH OF THE NEW WORLD WAS NOT GOLD
Pages 36-37

> *The men were anxious to find gold, but the wealth of the New World proved to be the plants, the animals, and the opportunity to enjoy the fruits of individual enterprise.*

● The islands and continents of the South have the largest and most beautiful plants and animals. How many different colors does a parrot have? What is unusual about parrots? The sailors and Columbus were interested in the new plants and animals, but what did they desire even more?

● How could Columbus communicate with the Indians when he couldn't speak their language? How did they speak to him?

● Look at the picture and locate the ships, then find Columbus and one of the sailors "talking" to the Indians.

COLUMBUS'S FIRST COLONY NEEDED SELF-GOVERNMENT
Pages 38-39

> *No matter what happened or how discontented the men became, Columbus continued to trust that God had arranged everything for the best.*

● The Bible teaches how each individual should be treated. God created each person and made each one very special. How did Columbus's actions show that he thought every man was important?

- How were these islands different from the other islands? Find Cuba and Haiti on a map.

- How did Columbus believe that God had arranged everything for the best?

- Did the men treat the Indians well after Columbus was gone? Why not?

- Review the definition of self-government. Did the men have self-government? How did this affect their relationship with the Indians?

COLUMBUS RETURNED AS A HERO
Pages 40-41

> *God enabled Columbus to achieve the great voyage across the ocean with safety and success.*

- How did Columbus show great courage on the trip back to Spain? How did God protect him?

- How did Columbus try to preserve a record of his explorations? Why?

- What riches did Columbus show to the people of Spain? How was Spain very different for the Indians?

- What did the King of Portugal think about Columbus's plan now?

COLUMBUS'S REWARD FOR HIS HARD WORK
Pages 42-43

> *At last Columbus was honored and rewarded for his sacrifices, patience, courage, and commitment.*

- How was Columbus rewarded for the success of his voyage?

- In the picture, what does Columbus have in his hand? How did he obtain it? Why are the Indians wrapped in blankets? What can be seen that is almost like the royal flag?
  Columbus could not take the King and Queen to the islands he had found, and he could not take pictures of what he had found, so the best thing he could do was bring some of his discoveries back to Spain.

STUDENT ACTIVITIES

- Have the students color a picture of Columbus claiming the New World for Spain.

- Find a picture for the students to color, showing Columbus presenting the story of his voyage to King Ferdinand and Queen Isabella.

- Take the students outside and have them imagine what it was like for Columbus to sail without knowing exactly where he was going. Establish a location to represent Spain and help the students use the compass to move west. Review the main events of leaving Spain and the first weeks of the voyage.

- Bring a spyglass or binoculars for the students to use. Help them to see faraway details, such as a bird's nest, a distant sign, etc. This will help the students imagine how excited the sailors were to know they were near the land.

- *Suggested Student Activities*, #9-15, q.v. p. 107-108.

Section VI

"MAN PROPOSES, GOD DISPOSES"

LEADING IDEAS

THE SECOND VOYAGE WAS MUCH EASIER THAN THE FIRST
Pages 44-45

> *Now that he knew the way, the voyage across the ocean was much easier for Columbus, the sailors, the King and Queen, and their families.*

- Why was it easier to find sailors who wanted to go on the second voyage?

- Who went with Columbus on this voyage? How did that encourage him?

- Contrast the departure for the first and second voyage.

- How were Columbus's new discoveries different from those of the first voyage? Point out the islands which he found on this voyage.

- Count the number of ships for this voyage. Find the Indians who wanted to kill the Spaniards.

- Why were the men so disappointed on this voyage?

- How had the greed for gold become harmful to the men who stayed at the fort? Why were the actions of the sailors wrong?

DIFFICULTIES PROVED COLUMBUS'S STRENGTH
Pages 46-47

> *The steadfastness, patience, and perseverance which enabled Columbus to spend years working to find assistance, once again enabled him to stand firm in his intended purpose.*

- How did people of Spain hurt Columbus while he was away? Were the things they said true? What should people remember before they say unkind or false things? How did King Ferdinand and Queen Isabella show that they still liked Columbus's ideas, but no longer trusted him? Had Columbus done anything to deserve that treatment?

- Why was it hard for Columbus to find a crew? Would these sailors be harder or easier to lead on the voyage? Why?

- Use a map to find the Orinoco River where Columbus arrived on his third voyage. Why wasn't Columbus pleased?

- The lies about Columbus encouraged wicked men to be even more cruel. Who really wanted to rule the islands? A traitor is a person who does something to hurt his

51

country. Was Columbus truly a traitor? Why was it wise for him to not allow his friends to fight for his freedom?

● How had Columbus changed on the outside? How had he stayed the same on the inside?

GOD'S PLAN FOR COLUMBUS WAS BEST
Pages 48-49

> *Columbus had many great plans and hopes for his life. He was Providentially prevented from accomplishing some of those plans, Providentially protected from harm, and long afterward honored for having made a discovery of which he had not even dreamed.*

● If Columbus had been permitted to rule the islands, would he have been able to make other voyages? How was this part of God's plan? How did God use Columbus's sickness to help him?

● Even though Columbus had successfully found land to the West, he still had difficulty raising the resources for his voyage. What character quality kept him from giving up?

● What character quality enabled Columbus to continue directing the voyage even though he was sometimes very sick?

● Show the students pictures of hurricanes. Can people be as strong as a hurricane? Who gives hurricanes their power? Lead the students to reflect upon the tremendous power of God and His wonderful love which protects even during storms and dangers. Review related Bible passages or stories and appropriate songs or poetry.

FACING DISCOURAGEMENT WITH COURAGE
Pages 50-51

> *As the leader, Columbus had to make difficult decisions and continue his efforts. A weaker man might have given up, but Columbus's inner strength upheld him once again during overwhelming discouragement.*

● What problems did Columbus and his men have?

● What men showed excellent courage and bravery?

● How did God take care of the men when their food ran out? How did He prove that He must be trusted to care for each individual?

COLUMBUS'S IMAGINATION HELPED AGAIN
Pages 52-53

> *Columbus's knowledge and ingenuity were again helpful in preserving the lives of the men. God's Providence in protecting the men in the canoe and the subsequent rescue is unquestionable.*

● How did Columbus know there would be an eclipse? Why were the Indians ignorant about God and about the wonders of His creation? How can God's Providence be seen during this time? How did Columbus show his unselfishness?

COLUMBUS LED OTHERS TO THE NEW WORLD
Pages 54-55

> *Columbus was Providentially prepared and directed to discover new lands and lead others to them.*

● Why did God allow Columbus to sail before the Portuguese had found a different way to the East? Why was the American continent a help to Columbus?

> *The character qualities of the great explorer provide an example to be followed today—love of learning, imagination, perseverance, faith and steadfastness, courage, and respect for others.*

● How did the other sea captains know how to sail across the Atlantic? How did Columbus show others that he was the leader of the explorers?

REMEMBERING CHRISTOPHER COLUMBUS
Pages 56-57

> *Christopher Columbus is to be remembered as the first to sail across the Atlantic and link the Old World to the New World.*

● Why was Genoa the right place for Christopher to be born and grow up? Columbus wanted to find China and India. Instead, what other place did Columbus find? Why was this discovery important in God's plan?

STUDENT ACTIVITIES

● Discuss the differences between salt water and fresh water. Prepare small pictures of animals which live only in fresh water and other animals which live only in salt water. Prepare a separate page with two columns labelled salt water and fresh water. As the students cut out the pictures, discuss the animals individually and have the students glue the pictures under the proper category.

● Using black and white construction paper, prepare pictures of the moon in different stages of an eclipse. Have the students cut out the pictures of the moon and glue them on the black paper in order.

● Sing appropriate songs describing God as Creator and reflecting His power over His creation.

● Read to the class the poem, "It Couldn't be Done," by Edgar A. Guest. Commit all or portions of the poem to memory.

CONCLUSION

In teaching any unit of study, the teacher should always allow time for a conclusion — not only a *closing* of the study, but an opportunity to reason with the students regarding the leading ideas that have been taught and to solidify their understanding of those ideas.

The teacher should be creative in preparing the review lessons for the students, not merely asking factual questions and having students respond in answers which do not require reasoning.

One method of review for students who are not yet able to read is for the teacher to show the students each of the pictures in the biography and ask leading questions to help the student remember the ideas that were taught corresponding to the various pictures.

The teacher might want to use a large map and locate the various places which were of importance in the life and adventures of Columbus. The students can then tell the stories of what happened in those locations and how God's Providence was shown, Columbus's character evidenced, etc.

Any pictures and maps that the students have prepared for their notebooks make good reminders of the ideas that were taught. If they have done several projects throughout the study of the biography, those pages may be used as a chronological review of Columbus's life and important events.

If the class has participated in various activities throughout the study (q.v. p. 107),

the teacher may wish to remind the students of the activity and ask them what lessons they learned and help them to again identify how that activity related to the study of the life of Columbus.

Following are suggestions for the types of questions which can be used to guide a class review of Columbus's life and accomplishments. The teacher may wish to revise these or write similar questions relating specifically to the leading ideas emphasized throughout the study of the biography.

- How did God prepare Columbus to be an explorer?

- Describe Columbus's character and how it helped him overcome obstacles.

- In what ways did Columbus show that he depended on God?

- Tell how self-government was necessary for the voyages and the colony.

- Columbus believed every individual was important. How did he show his beliefs in his treatment of his sailors and the Indians?

- What was Columbus's part on the Chain of Christianity?

PART V

MEET CHRISTOPHER COLUMBUS

by James T. de Kay

FIRST INSPIRATION OF COLUMBUS.
(From the statue by Giulio Monteverde, in the Museum of Fine Arts, Boston)

COLUMBUS AT THE CONVENT
[July, 1491]

Dreary and brown the night comes down,
    Gloomy, without a star.
On Palos town the night comes down;
The day departs with a stormy frown;
    The sad sea moans afar.

A convent-gate is near; 't is late;
    Ting-ling! the bell they ring.
They ring the bell, they ask for bread —
"Just for my child," the father said.
    Kind hands the bread will bring.

White was his hair, his mein was fair,
    His look was calm and great.
The porter ran and called a friar;
The friar made haste and told the prior;
    The prior came to the gate.

He took them in, he gave them food;
    The traveller's dreams he heard;
And fast the midnight moments flew,
And fast the good man's wonder grew,
    And all his heart was stirred.

The child the while, with soft, sweet smile,
    Forgetful of all sorrow,
Lay soundly sleeping in his bed.
The good man kissed him then, and said:
    "You leave us not to-morrow!

I pray you rest the convent's guest;
    The child shall be our own —
A precious care, while you prepare
Your business with the court, and bear
    Your message to the throne."

And so his guest he comforted.
    O wise, good prior! to you,
Who cheered the stranger's darkest days,
And helped him on his way, what praise
    And gratitude are due!

- John T. Trowbridge
Poems of American History
Houghton Mifflin Company, 1908

Section I

MEET CHRISTOPHER COLUMBUS
by James T. de Kay

Chapter 1

The effects of Christopher Columbus's explorations cannot be compared to any other geographic discoveries of the earth. They were unexpected, somewhat mysterious, and completely unanticipated—demonstrating the Divine power governing the affairs of men to advance His perfect plan.

"Christopher Columbus loved the sea. He loved travel and adventure. He dreamed of finding great riches in faraway lands.

"In 1492 he set out on his most famous voyage. His ships were battered by high winds and raging seas. He explored wild new lands. He met strange Indian tribes. Every day he faced great danger. But he never gave up.

"Christopher Columbus never heard the word 'America.' But his great voyage made him one of the most important men in American history."[19]

The biography by James T. de Kay offers a record of Columbus's life which the primary age student may read for himself.

Additional ideas and principles may be presented by the teacher to expand the material and include God's Providence and the principles of America's Christian History and Government.

Washington Irving's biography of Christopher Columbus provides a fine resource for the teacher's further understanding of the life and work of Columbus. Selected sections of Irving's work have been included for the teacher's consideration, q.v. p. 77.

LEADING IDEAS

When presenting each day's lesson, the teacher should have specific goals. The main goal should be to teach a leading idea through the reading, facts, discussion, and other class activities. *This leading idea is a conclusion to which the teacher should reason with the students.*

Leading ideas from the text are highlighted in boxes. Each teacher must determine the leading ideas to be emphasized with the students. Although numerous ideas have been identified, the teacher should not endeavor to be comprehensive of all these ideas, but must consider the age and capacity of the students.

> *God created Columbus with the unique interests, spirit, and abilities to be a sailor.*

● God's instruction to man was to subdue the earth and take dominion over it. In accordance with His timetable He raised up a

57

An American Christian Approach for Teaching

man to lead the way to the Western hemisphere for the advancement of the gospel and its outworkings in the New World.

"... Christopher Columbus was not afraid. His dream was to cross the Western Ocean. He became one of the greatest explorers in history." (page 7)

TOPICS FOR REFLECTION

Topics for reflection have been identified to inspire both teacher and student to reason concerning God's Providence in America's Christian history and government. Some topics are appropriate for class discussion, others for teacher consideration, and some for student written work.

● In order to be a leader, a person must have goals and dreams. What dream did Columbus have?

● To accomplish his goals, Columbus needed certain character qualities. What were they?

STUDENT ACTIVITIES

● Variety of presentation helps to preserve the interest of the students in whatever subject is being taught. Personalizing the lesson for each individual is particularly enjoyable. The poem on page 14 of this volume was written to a young girl as the introduction to a biog-

raphy of Columbus. To whet the student's appetite for the many adventures found in the text, this poem could be read with the students before they begin their study. Teachers might write each student's name in the title to make it more fun.

SAMPLE STUDENT NOTES
Chapters 1-3

FIRST GRADE STUDENTS

God's Providence in Columbus's Life

Columbus was born in Genoa, next to the Mediterranean Sea.
God protected Columbus when his ship sank.

FOR OLDER STUDENTS

God's Providence in Columbus's Life

Columbus was born in Genoa, Italy, next to the Mediterranean Sea. There he saw interesting ships from other countries.

God protected Columbus when his ship sank and brought him to the best country for learning about sailing.

58

Section II

HISTORIC AND GEOGRAPHIC SETTING

Chapter 2

LEADING IDEAS

> **The busy activities of a seaport intrigued Columbus and planted within him the desire to visit faraway places.**

● Columbus spent his childhood in the Providential revival of geographic interest. (*Irving*, q.v. p. 80)

"In the spring of 1476 there was some exciting news. Five ships were getting ready to leave Genoa. They were going to England. England is far away from Genoa. It is far away from the Mediterranean Sea. The ships would have to sail out on the great Western Ocean. Then they would sail north, past the lands of Spain, Portugal and France." (page 10)

● The setting in which an individual lives is an influence on his life, but his choices determine its course. (*Irving*, q.v. p. 80)

"About 500 years ago in the city of Genoa lived a red-haired boy. His name was Christopher Columbus. He worked for his father making cloth. But he did not want to

be a clothmaker all his life. He wanted to see new lands and have adventures. He wanted to be a sailor.

"Genoa was a good place to learn about sailing. It was a busy port on the Mediterranean Sea. Sailing ships from many lands came there." (page 8)

> **Christopher found the great desire of his heart fulfilled on board the ships where he became well-known as a master seaman.**

● Navigation was a rigorous school and the sea a demanding schoolmaster, causing Columbus to be a responsible youth. (*Irving*, q.v. p. 81)

"Christopher soon learned to sail. First he sailed in little boats just for the fun of it. Then he sailed on big ships. He learned all the things a sailor has to know. He learned to tell a forecastle from a poop deck. He learned about masts and sails and yards. He learned about cleats and rigging and all kinds of sea-going things.

"By the time Christopher was 25 years old, he had sailed all over the Mediterranean Sea. . . .

"Christopher's wish had come true. He was a sailor." (pages 9-10)

TOPICS FOR REFLECTION

● How did Genoa influence Columbus's chosen occupation and prepare him to fulfill it?

● Who arranged Columbus's life so that these influences could be in place? Why?

STUDENT ACTIVITIES

In addition to reading, relating, reasoning, and recording, a variety of related activities should be included to bring enjoyment to the study. These activities should correspond to the material being studied and increase the student's understanding. A number of student activities have been suggested for consideration.

● A map is a necessary tool for relating historic events to their geographic locations. It also enables the student to see the scope of Columbus's adventures. The students should master the geographic setting of Columbus's boyhood through preparing a map of Italy, showing important locations, including Genoa and the surrounding waterways. See page 272 of *A Guide to American Christian Education for the Home and School*, published by the American Christian History Institute, for specific instructions regarding map work.

● If possible, visit a museum in which rope-making or sailing are illustrated. If this is not possible, check with libraries, etc., for videos, pictures, or diagrams showing the skills and excitement of sailing.

● Identify the "ingredients" of a good sailor.

● Identify the ways in which sailing was controlled by the weather.

● Find enjoyable songs about sailing for the children to learn. These can be sung periodically throughout the entire study.

● *Suggested Student Activities,* #1, q.v. p. 107.

BULLETIN BOARD SUGGESTION

Prepare a large diagram of a ship, including the detailed information identified on pages 9 and 30-31, of the *Meet Christopher Columbus* biography. Throughout the study of the voyage, have the students refer to the diagram to clarify the descriptions of the ships and sailing. The students will benefit from learning to observe details and relate them to their study.

Section III

PROVIDENTIAL PRESERVATION AND PLACEMENT

Chapter 3

LEADING IDEA

> ***In some of his darkest and most difficult hours, God was bringing Columbus to exactly the right place.***

● Columbus was prepared for adventure on his first voyage out into the Western Ocean, but he did not realize the life-changing effects it would have. The desperate effort to preserve his own life brought Columbus to the heart of navigational activities in Portugal. (*Irving*, q.v. p. 81)

"At last, late at night, he reached land. He pulled himself up on the beach and rested. Some men came down to help him. They told him he was in the country of Portugal." (page 13)

TOPICS FOR REFLECTION

"PROGRESS OF DISCOVERY UNDER PRINCE HENRY OF PORTUGAL"

In the fifteenth century, Prince Henry had led his nation to the forefront of navigational activities. Washington Irving recorded the distinct contributions of Prince Henry. Although this contribution is not included in *Meet Christopher Columbus*, God's Providence is specifically evident and the teacher may wish to include Prince Henry as part of the study. (*Irving*, q.v. p. 81)

● Why did it please God to preserve Columbus's life?

● What qualities of character enabled Columbus to swim for many hours during the night until he finally reached shore?

● How is a belief in Providential protection supported and illustrated in the Bible?

STUDENT ACTIVITIES

● Sing songs centered around God's protection.

● Prepare a map of Europe for the students to outline and label. Include Italy as the birthplace of Columbus and Portugal as the country which enhanced his education. As the story continues, additional countries may be identified according to their contribution to Columbus's life.

● Commit a Bible promise of Divine protection to memory, i.e. Psalm 4:8, Proverbs 18:10, Psalm 121:7.

SAMPLE STUDENT NOTES

Chapters 1-3

Columbus's Character	Examples
Steadfastness	Columbus never gave up.
Courage	Columbus was not afraid to sail where no one had gone before.
Diligence	Columbus was a sailor by age fourteen and a captain when he was a young man.

Section IV

THE MANHOOD OF COLUMBUS

Chapters 4-6

LEADING IDEAS

> *Long before Columbus was born, adventurous men such as Leif Erikson, Marco Polo, and others had set off by land and sea for unknown places. Their examples encouraged Columbus to undertake his enterprise to the Indies.*

> *In some of Columbus's darkest and most difficult hours, God was working to lead him to exactly the right place.*

Limited knowledge, serious consideration, and Divine Providence brought Columbus to produce a daring plan. Columbus's son, Ferdinand, identified three specific premises upon which Columbus established his great theory: 1) The Nature of Things, 2) The Authority of Learned Writers, and 3) The Reports of Navigators. (*Irving*, q.v. p. 83)

"Columbus was sure he could find a way. He studied maps. He read books about the Indies. One book he read over and over was called 'The Adventures of Marco Polo.'" (pages 16-17)

"From reading Marco Polo's book, Columbus tried to figure out how to get to the Indies. Marco Polo got there by going around the world to the east. Columbus knew the world was round. So he knew he could get there by going around the world the other way--to the west." (page 18)

● Columbus arrived in Portugal as a successful seaman, and was Providentially led to acquaintance with a leading family. ("The Manhood of Columbus," *Irving*, q.v. p. 82)

"Christopher Columbus decided to stay in Portugal. He went to live near the big busy port of Lisbon. He married. He and his wife had a baby boy. . . ." (page 14)

● Portugal exercised a vast influence on Columbus, but was not destined to accept his plan for exploration. ("Events in Portugal," *Irving*, q.v. p. 84)

"The King's advisors studied the plan. They said they did not like it. They said that Columbus was wrong. They said that the Western Ocean was bigger than Columbus thought. It would take too long to cross it. A ship could not hold enough food for such a long voyage.

"The King listened to his advisors. He told Columbus he would not give him the ships." (pages 19-20)

> *Columbus waited many years, and suffered poverty and disappointment; but in God's perfect time, friends were raised up to help him along the path to success.*

• God prepares individuals, then He causes events.

• Columbus was Providentially directed to the individuals best suited to promote his cause. (*Irving*, q.v. p. 85)
"In Seville, Columbus talked to a rich man named Don Luis de la Cerda. Don Luis liked the plan. He said that he would give Columbus the ships for the voyage.

"Don Luis thought he should tell Queen Isabella of Spain about the plan. He wrote to her. She was very interested. She asked Columbus to come and tell her more about it. . . ." (pages 20-21)

• Columbus's plans for exploration gained credibility because of his own character. (*Irving*, q.v. p. 86)

• Columbus was forced to overcome errors, prejudices, and ignorance to gain favor for his idea. (*Irving*, q.v. p. 87)

• When Columbus had reached the limit of his patience, God placed another influential individual in his path to encourage him. (*Irving*, q.v. p. 87)

• Queen Isabella was the lady of inspiration and vision whose ideals matched the cause of Columbus and brought her to become his patron. (*Irving*, q.v. p. 89)
"Columbus went to Palos to pick up Diego. There he got a letter. It was from Isabella. She wanted to see him! Columbus got on a mule. He rode quickly off to see the Queen.

"This time Isabella had wonderful news. She said she would help him." (pages 24-25)

TOPICS FOR REFLECTION

• How were the "times prepared for the men" who would advance the fields of navigation and discovery? (Think in terms of individuals, events, inventions, etc.)

• Individuals who propose new and daring plans must be prepared for lonely leadership. How did the Portuguese king's rejection of Columbus's plan affect Columbus?

• How can the idea that an individual must rely solely on God and not on man be identified in Scripture? How does it relate to Columbus's experiences?

• Describe the Providential influences which prepared Spain for Columbus's enterprise to the Indies.

• How was Columbus Providentially directed to the appropriate individuals who would take an interest in his cause?

• Identify the means by which God used specific individuals to help forward the Chain of Christianity.

• How is character defined? How is it formed in the life of the individual? What influences had operated in Columbus's life to produce his character? How did his own personal character determine the outcome of his plans for sailing to the Indies?

• How did the response from the Council at Salamanca prove that education and enterprise go hand in hand? (*Irving*, q.v. p. 87)

- Describe Columbus's view of his plan in terms of Providential history.

- How was Columbus able to remain true to his ideas when the opposition was so strong?

- Contrast decision-making by whim and decision-making by principle. Give evidence of the method Columbus used.

- Columbus felt the full responsibility for seeing his plan become a reality. How did this influence his actions?

- What qualities of Columbus's character caused the King and Queen to respect his ideas?

- How had Friar Perez been Providentially prepared to meet a need in Columbus's life and vision? Define patriotism and Biblically research its ideas. How did the friar's patriotism govern his actions and benefit his country?

  How do these events prove that one individual can dramatically change the course of history? (*Irving*, q.v. p. 88)

- By what qualifications does a man acquire property?

- Research the principle, "Conscience is the Most Sacred of All Property," using *Teaching and Learning America's Christian History* and *The Christian History of the Constitution*.

  Columbus's idea of crossing the Atlantic to reach the Indies was his property. He had invested vast amounts of time and effort to achieve its accomplishment. How did the terms of this agreement remunerate him for his efforts? ("Terms of Agreement," *Irving*, q.v. p. 89)

STUDENT ACTIVITIES

- Have students prepare a map identifying the travel route of Marco Polo, including the land of the Arabs, Cathay, India, and other locations mentioned in this section of the text.

- *Suggested Student Activities*, #2-5, q.v. p. 107.

SAMPLE STUDENT WORK

Chapters 4-6

The following sample questions illustrate the types of written work which the students could complete. These questions would be assigned as the material is taught. First grade students could be required to answer one to two questions in one assignment.

- In what ways did Portugal help Columbus, even though the King didn't provide the ships Columbus needed?

- When the King said "no," how did Columbus show steadfastness?

(Sample Student Work Continued)

- Columbus may have felt lonely. Who helped Columbus not be discouraged?

- What promise from God can help us never to be afraid when we are alone?

- How did God help Columbus receive permission to see Queen Isabella?

- On two different occasions Columbus was ready to leave Spain. How did God keep him from leaving each time?

- Why did Columbus deserve to be rewarded if his voyage succeeded?

BULLETIN BOARD SUGGESTION

Books to tell about far-away places.

A home near the ocean, so he could learn to sail.

A love of adventure.

God Provided for Columbus

A King and Queen to help him in his adventure.

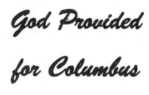

A just reward for his accomplishment.

A knowledge of sailing.

Ships and sailors for exploring.

Section V

CHRISTOPHER COLUMBUS'S GREAT ADVENTURE

Chapters 7-11

LEADING IDEAS

> *Columbus waited many years, and suffered poverty and disappointment; but in God's perfect time, friends were raised up to help him along the path to success.*

- Columbus was Providentially directed to the individuals best suited to promote his cause. (*Irving*, q.v. p. 89)

  "One of the first men he saw was a sailor named Martin Alonso Pinzon. Pinzon was a thin, hungry-looking man. He was a friend of Columbus.

  "Pinzon said he wanted to sail with Columbus. Columbus was glad to have him. . . ."(page 27)

- Queen Isabella sent orders to the town of Palos requiring them to furnish two armed caravels for Columbus's expedition. (*Irving*, q.v. p. 89)

  "The Queen told the town of Palos to give Columbus two ships. They were called caravels. They were fast and easy to sail. Their names were the Nina and the Pinta." (pages 27-28)

> *Columbus recorded the Providential Acts of God throughout his life.*

- Columbus recognized the importance of recording the events and observations of the voyage, and diligently set out to do so. (*Irving*, q.v. p. 90)

  "Columbus wrote down everything that happened during the voyage. He wrote about the weather. He wrote about the stars and the winds. He wrote about strange fish that swam around his ship. He wrote about the birds that flew overhead. Often he worked far into the night. Sometimes he did not sleep at all." (pages 36-37)

> *God Providentially encouraged Columbus through signs that land was ahead, and Columbus in turn was responsible for keeping his men on course and helping them to maintain their strong hope.*

- God's Providence was evident during many difficult days. (*Irving*, q.v. p. 92)

"Every day they saw more and more birds. This made Columbus happy. He was sure these were land birds. It must mean that land was near. . . ." (page 40)

> *After long weeks of sailing, land was sighted at last, and God allowed the crew to arrive safely.*

• The vision for which Columbus had labored during years of opposition and discouragement was at last achieved. (*Irving*, q.v. p. 96)

"And sure enough, land it was. The next morning Columbus sailed around the land. He saw it was an island. The hills and trees were beautiful. The air was filled with the smell of flowers. The sailors could see people on the island. The people wore no clothes.

They came down to the beach to see the ships." (page 43)

> *All were happy to have arrived on the beautiful shore, where Columbus thanked the Lord for their safe voyage and claimed the land for Spain.*

• "A man's heart deviseth his way: but the Lord directeth his steps." Proverbs 16:9. Columbus's plans for exploration were Divinely inspired, adjusted, and controlled. (*Irving*, q.v. p. 97)

"The sailors rowed Columbus to the shore. He stepped onto the beach. He got down on his knees and said a prayer of thanks.

"Columbus named the island San Salvador. He said it now belonged to Ferdinand and Isabella." (page 43)

TOPICS FOR REFLECTION

• How were the remaining obstacles to the voyages Providentially overcome?

• Describe the methods by which the crown provided support for the enterprise. What philosophy of government is evident? How did this affect the citizens of Spain? How did it affect Columbus's efforts?

• What evidence is given in Columbus's journal to prove that he had a strong education?

• How can Providential protection be seen in the situation with the Pinta's broken rudder? ("Providential Beginnings," *Irving*, q.v. p. 90)

• Describe Columbus's character in dealing with the fears of his sailors.

• What dangers did Columbus face in endeavoring to sail away from the Canary Islands and how were they Providentially overcome?

• Voluntary consent is the basis on which American enterprise and government is established. How did Columbus suffer because his voyage was not established on voluntary consent?

• How did Columbus endeavor to gain the voluntary consent of his sailors? His efforts bear testimony to the fact that the vision of any endeavor must rest in the heart of its leadership and consistently be expressed to the whole. It is interesting to note the Scripture, "Where there is no vision, the people perish." (Proverbs 29:18) Compare Columbus's style of leadership with the leadership of Moses, Joshua, David, Christ, etc.

- Washington Irving and James de Kay each describe the two reckonings made by Columbus. In reality the public reckoning was a more accurate calculation of the number of miles travelled. How can God's Providence be seen in the entire situation? Consider: Man proposes, but God disposes. (*Irving*, q.v. p. 92)

- All of man's enterprise rests upon an understanding of the fixed principles with which the sovereign God created the universe. How did the fear of the men reflect this need?

- What testimony is given of Columbus's character?

- For teacher consideration: describe Washington Irving's view of God, man, and science.

- In what ways were the signs of land a source of discouragement to the sailors? How could they be considered a Providential source of encouragement? What comparisons can be made to the Israelites as they travelled toward the Promised Land?

- Christopher Columbus possessed tremendous internal confidence in his plans to discover land. Because of this he was not swayed by external circumstances—either positive or negative. How did he endeavor to convey this to the crew? Why were they unable to possess the same internal confidence?

- As much as possible, Columbus endeavored to lead his sailors by persuading them to agree with his choices. When this was no longer possible, what arguments did he use? How does this reveal the view of man and government which was prevalent at the time?

- How did Columbus's understanding of God's Principle of Individuality affect his relationship to the men?

STUDENT ACTIVITIES

- Have the students keep a journal of daily activities according to the style which Columbus used. Specify a certain number of days or weeks in which this journal will be kept and have the students turn it in at the conclusion of that time. This exercise will serve to sharpen observation and writing skills, and will emphasize the importance of written records in preserving one's heritage, both individually and nationally.

- Have students prepare a map identifying the route of Columbus's first voyage.

- List the many preparations which had to be made before Columbus and his fleet could sail. This could be a class activity or individual student project.

- *Suggested Student Activities*, #6-12, q.v. p. 107.

TIMELINES

To provide students with a more complete understanding of history, teachers should identify the historic setting of events on the Chain of Christianity. Timelines provide a concise representation of events in chronological order and allow the students to comprehend a series of events rather than learning about isolated instances and occurrences which have no relation to one another.

Timelines also provide a visible record of events which can be used to review key ideas presented to the class.

For the primary students, timelines should be simple and brief. The teacher may wish to do several timelines throughout the study, keeping each one short enough to finish in one lesson.

The following sample timelines comprehend the material found in Chapters 7-11 and could be used to review key ideas which have been taught. The addition of small illustrations by the students would provide an enjoyable opportunity to exercise their drawing abilities and will enhance the timelines.

COLUMBUS'S ADVENTURE

FIRST GRADE STUDENTS

August 3, 1492   The ships left Palos.

They sailed West many miles.

October 12, 1492   Columbus saw land.

OLDER STUDENTS

August 3, 1492   Columbus and his crew left Palos in ships — the Nina, Pinta, and Santa Maria.

They sailed West into the Atlantic Ocean, and soon were out of sight of land.

October 12, 1492   Land was finally seen, and the men thanked God for His protection and guidance.

Section VI

GOD'S PROVIDENCE EVIDENT DURING DIFFICULT DAYS

Chapters 12-16

LEADING IDEAS

> *Christopher Columbus was a man with extraordinary strength of character which enabled him to accomplish great things. The character of others involved in the enterprise, however, sometimes led to difficulties and dangers.*

• The success of any enterprise or endeavor rests upon the character of the individuals involved. (*Irving*, q.v. p. 98)

• Divine Providence granted the wisdom, protection, and encouragement needed for the unique challenges of the return voyage.

Indian Encounter:
(*Irving*, q.v. p. 99)

"The ships sailed on to the east. In a few days they came to a small bay. Some of the men went ashore to find food. Suddenly more than 50 Indians jumped out from behind the trees. They had bows and arrows. They attacked the men. The men fought back. . . .

"The Indians were surprised by the bravery of Columbus's men. They dropped their bows and ran away." (pages 55-56)

Return Voyage:
(*Irving*, q.v. p. 100)

"For almost a month the trip went well. Then the wind grew stronger. It turned into a gale. The ships rolled and tossed in a great storm. Waves washed over the decks. Ropes and sails were torn away . . .

"The storm did not let up. The men were terrified. They cried out to God for help." (page 56)

Sighting Land:
(*Irving*, q.v. p. 101)

"Another terrible day passed. Then the wind died down. And at last, far away, the men saw an island." (page 57)

• Success brought Columbus both benefits and dangers. (*Irving* q.v. p. 101)

"The captain told Columbus that the sailors were prisoners. He said the island belonged to Portugal. The Spanish had no right to be there . . . He told Columbus to sail to shore.

"Columbus knew that the captain would take him prisoner, too. He yelled out that someday he would come back and punish him.

"At last the captain gave in. If he could not get Columbus, he did not care about the other men. He let them go. When they were back on the Nina, Columbus sailed away." (page 60)

• Columbus's ability to discern potential danger and his wisdom enabled him to steer through the difficulties with Portugal. (*Irving*, q.v. p. 101)

"Soon the King of Portugal sent for Columbus. Columbus did not want to go. Twice he had asked this king for ships. And twice this king had turned him down. But Columbus did not dare say no to a King.

"Columbus took some gold. He took some Indians he had brought back. He went to see the King.

"He told the King he had found the Indies. He showed him the gold. He showed him the Indians. He said they were very clever people." (pages 62-63)

TOPICS FOR REFLECTION

• The stated objectives for Columbus's expedition included both evangelization and the discovery of wealth. Why was the financial gain necessary in order to achieve evangelization?

• Throughout Columbus's voyages and the initial settlement in North America, individuals were driven to search for gold, bypassing the rich natural resources which proved to be the first financial wealth from the New World. The Plymouth Colony was the first colony to concentrate on natural resources rather than searching for gold. How does this reflect the influence of Christianity?

• Just as the Pilgrims hoped to be stepping-stones to others for propagating and advancing the gospel in the New World, how was Columbus one of the stepping-stones in that process? What individuals did God eventually raise up in the New World to concentrate their efforts in the evangelization of the Indians?

• How did Pinzon's departure from the leadership of Columbus reflect the importance of unity in achieving union?

• Contrast the relationship between Columbus and Pinzon at the beginning of the enterprise and at this point.

• How does Columbus's description of the islands reflect the individuality of the southern continents as the continents of nature? (*Irving*, q.v. p. 97)

• Describe the efforts and character demanded of Columbus in order to successfully carry out this voyage.

• Identify the consequences upon the entire company of men when a few individuals failed to exercise self-government.

• Give examples of God's Providential protection of the crew both during and after the shipwreck.

• Why did many of the sailors desire to stay on the island?

• Identify the significance of the name "La Navidad." Note: The shipwreck occurred off the shore of the island on Christmas Eve. (*Irving*, q.v. p. 98) The wood from the wreck was used for building the fort.

• What positive and negative effects were evidenced when the Nina and Pinta were reunited?

• Analyze Pinzon's character as he made excuses for his actions and Columbus's character in responding to the difficulty.

- How did lack of trust between the Indians and the sailors cause difficulties to occur? How did Columbus's actions reflect Christian ideas?

- Why was it Providential that the most difficult sailing occurred on the way home, rather than on the way to the Indies?

- How did Columbus show wisdom and justice in his dealings with the Portuguese governor?

- How did the events of his arrival in Portugal reconfirm for Columbus that Providence had directed him to receive support from Spain rather than Portugal as he made his voyages of discovery?

- A written record of firsthand experiences is an invaluable source by which a nation's history may be maintained. How did Columbus's actions prove that he understood this? Why are these writings so valuable today?

STUDENT ACTIVITIES

- Students may be encouraged to build a fort using wooden building blocks. Consider: Why was the fort necessary? How could the fort provide maximum protection? How did the character of the men and their actions toward the Indians negate any benefits provided by the fort?

    Since the text does not include these difficulties, see the complete *The Life and Voyages of Christopher Columbus*, by Washington Irving, or Josephine Pollard's biography, *Christopher Columbus and the Discovery of the New World*, published by Pilgrim Institute.

- *Suggested Student Activities*, #13, q.v. p. 107.

Section VII

"TO CASTILE AND LEON COLUMBUS GAVE A NEW WORLD"

Chapters 17-19

LEADING IDEAS

> **The Providential Hand of God in the opening of the New World.**

• Columbus's hardy genius, inflexible constancy, and heroic courage brought the ends of the earth into communication with each other.

"Soon other men were sailing west across the ocean. One of them was a man named Amerigo Vespucci. He decided that Columbus had not been to islands in the Indies after all. He said Columbus had found something even more important than a new way to the Indies. He had found new lands no one had ever heard of. He had found a whole 'new world.'" (page 70)

• "Western Europe received all the wisdom and experience of the ancient world . . . and her children, rich in her experience, instructed at once by her success and her mistakes, and aided always by her wisdom, found (let us hope) in America the goal of their noblest aspirations."[20]

> **Great deeds are accomplished by individuals who are willing to give up their time, their property, and sometimes even their lives.**

• The degree of difficulty barring one's path to success is directly related to the height of honor when the enterprise is accomplished. (*Irving*, q.v. p. 102)

• Columbus requested a title indicative of his authority and leadership as an explorer. The magnitude of his discoveries entitled him to the esteem and honor of men and nations for generations. (*Irving*, q.v. p. 103)

"Columbus stayed in Palos for two weeks. Then he went on to Seville. He had a wonderful time in Seville. People gave great parties for him. Everyone wanted to meet him. He was the hero of Spain." (pages 66-67)

"A week later Columbus set out for the city of Barcelona. He was going to see the king and queen." (page 68)

TOPICS FOR REFLECTION

• Compare the life of Martin Alonzo Pinzon to that of a Bible character. (Consider Jacob, Samson, Balaam, etc.)

• Describe the lessons which may be drawn from Pinzon's life. How does his entire relationship with Columbus prove that one must always place his confidence in God rather than in individuals?

• How did the prominent religion of Europe influence the Spanish nation as well as Columbus?

• How was Columbus's Christian character evident when he was honored for his success?

• Describe how God Providentially led many nations to aid Columbus in his efforts of exploration.

• How did God begin immediately planting the seed for England, a nation which would possess great Biblical reasoning, to be inspired for the future exploration and colonization of North America?

• Contrast the character of King Ferdinand and Queen Isabella. Consider their reasons for helping Columbus, their responses to the attitudes and actions of those who opposed Columbus, etc.

STUDENT ACTIVITIES

• Using a map of Spain, identify the cities to which Columbus traveled when he returned triumphantly, i.e., Palos, Seville, Barcelona.

• *Suggested Student Activities*, #14, q.v. p. 108.

CONCLUSION

For any unit of study, the teacher should always allow time for a conclusion — not only a *closing* of the study, but an opportunity to reason and solidify with the students the leading ideas that have been taught.

There are many methods which may be used for review. Although some facts should be included, the leading ideas are key to the students understanding of Providential history. The teacher might use maps, pictures in the text, or timelines to review the leading ideas and key events which have been covered. The students could write a short essay describing a particular aspect of the study of Columbus, including such topics as — Why was Columbus called the "Hero of Spain?" How

did Columbus earn the title, "Admiral of the Ocean Sea?"

Suggested questions for class discussion:

• History shows how God uses men and nations to accomplish His plan. Name two individuals and two nations used by God to help Columbus reach the New World. Describe the contributions of each.

• Columbus needed strong character to lead the explorations. How did he learn courage and steadfastness?

• What was Columbus's part on the Chain of Christianity?

PART VI

WASHINGTON IRVING

WASHINGTON IRVING.

THE ARMS OF COLUMBUS.

The True Story of Christopher Columbus
by Elbridge S. Brooks
D. Lothrop Company, ©1892

PILGRIM INSTITUTE

THE LIFE AND VOYAGES
OF
CHRISTOPHER COLUMBUS

by Washington Irving

Washington Irving entered the American stage during the early days of the republic, and made his mark as the first professional American writer. He can truly be considered the "Father of American Letters" as he "laid a broad foundation for all subsequent writing in America."[21]

A warm, sentimental, cheerful, humorous spirit influenced all of his writing. He sensed the romance and legend of the places he visited and successfully communicated those themes to the reader, touching the heartstring through the lives of the characters and the times in which they lived. His rich imagination came to life under the pen names he adopted, Jonathan Oldstyle, Launcelot Langstaff, Diedrich Knickerbocker, and Geoffrey Crayon.

Due to business efforts and political appointments, Irving spent seventeen years in Europe and discovered the wealth of Old World history. He found pleasure in recording his observations, which were so successful that he was welcomed by the leading writers of Europe, including Sir Walter Scott, establishing himself and his nation in the field of literature.

Irving's historic writings include the lives of both Christopher Columbus and George Washington, for whom he had been named. At the age of five he had been presented to Washington and was later inspired by the childhood memory to write about the Father of Our Country. During his visit to Spain, 1826-1829, Irving uncovered the treasures of romantic history awaiting the touch of a writer's pen. The objective of The Life and Voyages of Christopher Columbus *was "to relate the deeds and fortunes of the mariner who first had the judgment to divine, and the intrepidity to brave the mysteries of this perilous deep; and who, by his hardy genius, his inflexible constancy, and his heroic courage, brought the ends of the earth into communication with each other. The narrative of his troubled life is the link which connects the history of the old world with that of the new."[22]*

The Life and Voyages of Christopher Columbus *remains a leading, authentic resource based on original source documents. His insights assist the reader in discerning how greatly the discovery rested upon the direction of Providence, the monumental character of Columbus, and the Biblical ideas of men and nations on which the American republic was founded.*

"...As far as authenticated history extends, nothing was known of terra firma, and the islands of the western hemisphere, until their discovery toward the close of the fifteenth century. A wandering bark may occasionally have lost sight of the landmarks of the old continents, and been driven by tempests across the wilderness of waters long before the invention of the compass, but never returned to reveal the secrets of the ocean. And though, from time to time, some document has floated to the shores of the old world, giving its wondering inhabitants evidences of land far beyond their watery horizon; yet no one ventured to spread a sail, and seek that land enveloped in mystery and peril. Or if the legends of the Scandinavian voyagers be correct . . . they had but transient glimpses of the new world, leading to no certain or permanent knowledge, and in a little time lost again to mankind. Certain it is that at the beginning of the fifteenth century, when the most intelligent minds were seeking in every direction for the scattered lights of geographical knowledge, a profound ignorance prevailed among the learned as to the western regions of the Atlantic; its vast waters were regarded with awe and wonder, seeming to bound the world as with a chaos, into which conjecture could not penetrate, and enterprise feared to adventure. . . .

"Christopher Columbus, *Early Life* or Columbo, as the name is written in Italian, was born in the city of Genoa, about the year 1435. [Modern scholars date Columbus's birth at 1450.] He was the son of Dominico Columbo, a wool comber, and Susannah Fontanarossa, his wife, and it would seem that his ancestors had followed the same handicraft for several generations in Genoa. . . .

"Columbus was the oldest of four children; having two brothers, Bartholomew and Giacomo, or James (written Diego in Spanish), and one sister, of whom nothing is known but that she was married to a person in obscure life called Giacomo Bavarello. At a very early age Columbus evinced a decided inclination for the sea; his education, therefore, was mainly directed to fit him for maritime life, but was as general as the narrow means of his father would permit. Besides the ordinary branches of reading, writing, grammar and arithmetic, he was instructed in the Latin tongue, and made some proficiency in drawing and design. For a short time, also, he was sent to the university of Pavia, where he studied geometry, geography, astronomy and navigation. . . . according to his own account he entered upon a nautical life when but fourteen years of age.

"In tracing the early history of a man like Columbus, whose actions have had a vast effect on human affairs, it is interesting to notice how much has been owing to external influences, how much to an inborn propensity of the genius. In the latter part of his life, when, impressed with the sublime events brought about through his agency, Columbus looked back upon his career with a solemn and superstitious feeling, he attributed his early and irresistible inclination for the sea, and his passion for geographical studies, to an impulse from the Deity preparing him for the high decrees he was chosen to accomplish.

"The nautical propensity, however, evinced by Columbus in early life, is common to boys of enterprising spirit and lively imagination brought up in maritime cities; to whom the sea is the high road to adventure and the region of romance. Genoa, too, walled in and straitened on the land side by rugged mountains, yielded but little scope for enterprise on the shore, while an opulent and widely extended commerce, visiting every country, and a roving marine, battling in every sea, naturally led forth her children upon the waves, as their propitious element. . . .

"The strong passion for geographical knowl- *Geographic* edge, also, felt by Co- *Interest* lumbus in early life, and which inspired his after career, was incident to the age in which he lived. Geographical discovery was the brilliant path of light which was forever to distinguish the fifteenth century. . . .

"The knowledge thus reviving was limited and imperfect; yet, like the return of the morning light, it seemed to call a new creation into existence, and broke, with all the charm of wonder, upon imaginative minds. . . .

"Such was the state of information and feeling with *Influence* respect to this interesting *of Setting* science, in the early part of the fifteenth century. An interest still more intense was awakened by the discoveries which began to be made along the Atlantic coasts of Africa; and must have been particularly felt among a maritime and commercial people like the Genoese. To these circumstances may we ascribe the enthusiastic devotion which Columbus imbibed in his childhood for cosmographical studies, and which influenced all his after fortunes.

"The short time passed by him at the university of Pavia was barely sufficient to give him the rudiments of the necessary sciences; the familiar acquaintance with them, which he evinced in after life, must have been the result of diligent self-schooling, in casual hours of study amid the cares and vicissitudes of a rugged and wandering life. He was one of those men of strong natural genius, who, from having to contend at their very outset with privations and impediments, acquire an intrepidity in encountering and a facility in vanquishing difficulties, throughout their career. Such men learn to effect great purposes with small means, supplying this deficiency by the resources of their own energy and invention. This, from his earliest commencement, throughout the whole of his life, was one of the remarkable features in the history of Columbus. In every undertaking, the scantiness and apparent insufficiency of his means enhance the grandeur of his achievements.

Responsible Youth
"Columbus . . . commenced his nautical career when about fourteen years of age. . . .

"The seafaring life of the Mediterranean in those days was hazardous and daring. A commercial expedition resembled a warlike cruise, and the maritime merchant had often to fight his way from port to port. . . .

"Such was the rugged school in which Columbus was reared, and it would have been deeply interesting to have marked the early development of his genius amid its stern adversities. All this instructive era of his history, however, is covered with darkness. . . .

First voyage into the Western Ocean
". . . A desperate engagement took place; the vessels grappled each other, and the crews fought hand to hand, and from ship to ship. The battle lasted from morning until evening, with great carnage on both sides. The vessel commanded by Columbus was engaged with a huge Venetian galley. They threw hand-grenades and other fiery missiles, and the galley was wrapped in flames. The vessels were fastened together by chains and grappling irons, and could not be separated; both were involved in one conflagration, and soon became a mere blazing mass. The crews threw themselves into the sea; Columbus seized an oar, which was floating within reach, and being an expert swimmer, attained the shore, though full two leagues distant. It pleased God, says his son Fernando, to give him strength, that he might preserve him for greater things. After recovering from his exhaustion he repaired to Lisbon, where he found many of his Genoese countrymen, and was induced to take up his residence. . . .

Prince Henry
"The career of modern discovery had commenced shortly before the time of Columbus, and at the period of which we are treating was prosecuted with great activity by Portugal. . . .

"The grand impulse to discovery was not given by chance, but was the deeply meditated effort of one master mind. This was Prince Henry of Portugal . . . the character of this illustrious man, from whose enterprises the genius of Columbus took excitement, deserves particular mention.

"Having accompanied his father into Africa, in an expedition against the Moors at Ceuta he received much information concerning the coast of Guinea, and other regions in the interior, hitherto unknown to Europeans, and conceived an idea that important discoveries were to be made by navigating along the western coast of Africa. On returning to Portugal, this idea became his ruling thought. Withdrawing from the tumult of a court to a country retreat . . . in full view of the ocean, he drew around him men eminent in science, and prosecuted the study of those branches of knowledge connected with the maritime arts. . . .

"The Italians, or Lombards as they were called in the north of Europe, had long monopolized the trade of Asia. They had formed commercial establishments at Constantinople and in the Black Sea, where they received the rich produce of the Spice Islands, lying near the equator; and the silks, the gums, the perfumes,

81

the precious stones, and other luxurious commodities of Egypt and southern Asia, and distributed them over the whole of Europe.... All Europe was tributary to their commerce. Yet this trade had to pass through various intermediate hands, subject to the delays and charges of internal navigation, and the tedious and uncertain journeys of the caravan.... Thus, while the opulent traffic of the East was engrossed by these adventurous monopolists, the price of every article was enhanced by the great expense of transportation.

"It was the grand idea of Prince Henry, by circumnavigating Africa to open a direct and easy route to the source of this commerce, to turn it in a golden tide upon his country. He was, however, before the age in thought, and had to counteract ignorance and prejudice, and to endure the delays to which vivid and penetrating minds are subjected, from the tardy co-operations of the dull and the doubtful....

"To dispel these errors, and to give a scope to navigation equal to the grandeur of his designs, Prince Henry established a naval college, and erected an observatory at Sagres, and he invited thither the most eminent professors of the nautical faculties; ...

"The effects of this establishment were soon apparent. All that was known relative to geography and navigation was gathered together and reduced to system. A vast improvement took place in maps. The compass was also brought into more general use, especially among the Portuguese, rendering the mariner more bold and venturous, by enabling him to navigate in the most gloomy day and in the darkest night....

"Henry died ... without accomplishing the great object of his ambition.... however, [he] lived long enough to reap some of the richest rewards of a great and good mind. He beheld, through his means, his native country in a grand and active career of prosperity. The discoveries of the Portuguese were the wonder and admiration of the fifteenth century, and Portugal, from being one of the least among nations, suddenly rose to be one of the most important.

"All this was effected, not by arms, but by arts; not by the stratagems of a cabinet, but by the wisdom of a college. ...

"Henry, at his death, left it in charge to his country to prosecute the route to India ...The fame of the Portuguese discoveries, and of the expeditions continually setting out, drew the attention of the world. Strangers from all parts, the learned, the curious, and the adventurous, resorted to Lisbon to inquire into the particulars or to participate in the advantages of these enterprises. Among these was Christopher Columbus ...

"Columbus arrived at Lisbon about the year 1470. *Manhood* He was at that time in the full vigor of manhood, and of an engaging presence. Minute descriptions are given of his person. . . tall, well-formed, muscular, and of an elevated and dignified demeanor. His visage was long, and neither full nor meagre; his complexion fair and freckled, and inclined to ruddy; his nose aquiline; his cheek-bones were rather high, his eyes light gray, and apt to kindle; his whole countenance had an air of authority. His hair, in his youthful days, was of a light color; but care and trouble, ... soon turned it gray, and at thirty years of age it was quite white. He was moderate and simple in diet and apparel, eloquent in discourse, engaging and affable with strangers, and his amiableness and suavity in domestic life strongly attached his household to his person. His temper was naturally irritable; but he subdued it by the magnanimity of his spirit, comporting himself with a courteous and gentle gravity, and never indulging in any intemperance of language. Throughout his life he was noted for strict attention to the offices of religion, observing rigorously the fasts and ceremonies of the church; nor did his piety consist in mere forms, but partook of that lofty and solemn enthusiasm with which his whole character was strongly tinctured.

"While at Lisbon, he was accustomed to attend religious service at the chapel of the convent of All Saints. In this convent were certain ladies of rank ... With one of these Columbus became acquainted. She was Dona Felipa, daughter of Bartolomeo Monis de

Perestrello, an Italian cavalier, lately deceased who had been one of the most distinguished navigators under Prince Henry . . . The acquaintance soon ripened into attachment, and ended in marriage. . . .

"The newly married couple resided with the mother of the bride. The latter, perceiving the interest which Columbus took in all matters concerning the sea, related to him all she knew of the voyages and expeditions of her late husband, and brought him all his papers, charts, journals, and memorandums. In this way he became acquainted with the routes of the Portuguese, their plans and conceptions; and having, by his marriage and residence, become naturalized in Portugal, he sailed occasionally in the expeditions to the coast of Guinea. When on shore, he supported his family by making maps and charts. His narrow circumstances obliged him to observe a strict economy; yet we are told that he appropriated a part of his scanty means to the succor of his aged father at Genoa, and to the education of his younger brothers. . . .

"While his geographical labors thus elevated him to a communication with the learned, they were peculiarly calculated to foster a train of thoughts favorable to nautical enterprise. From constantly comparing maps and charts, and noting the progress and direction of discovery, he was led to perceive how much of the world remained unknown, and to meditate on the means of exploring it. His domestic concerns, and the connections he had formed by marriage, were all in unison with this vein of speculation. He resided for some time at the recently discovered island of Porto Santo, where his wife had inherited some property, and during his residence there she bore him a son, whom he named Diego. This residence brought him, as it were, on the very frontier of discovery. . . .

The Nature of Things

". . . The earth was a terraqueous sphere or globe, which might be travelled round from east to west, and that men stood foot to foot when on opposite points. The circumference from east to west, at the equator, Columbus divided . . . into twenty-four hours of fifteen degrees each, making three hundred and sixty degrees.

Of these he imagined . . . that fifteen hours had been known to the ancients . . . The Portuguese had advanced the western frontier one hour more by the discovery of the Azores and Cape de Verde Islands. There remained, then, according to the estimation of Columbus, eight hours, or one third of the circumference of the earth, unknown and unexplored. . . . Granting these premises, it was manifest that, by pursuing a direct course from east to west, a navigator would arrive at the extremity of Asia, and discover any intervening land.

". . . the authors . . . writings had weight in convincing him that the intervening ocean could be but of moderate expanse, and easy to be traversed. Among *Learned Writers* these, he cites the opinion of Aristotle, Seneca, and Pliny, that one might pass from Cadiz to the Indies in a few days; of Strabo, also, who observes, that the ocean surrounds the earth, bathing on the east the shores of India; on the west, the coasts of Spain and Mauritania; so that it is easy to navigate from one to the other on the same parallel.

"In corroboration of the idea that Asia, or, as he always terms it India, stretched far to the east, so as to occupy the greater part of the unexplored space, the narratives are cited of Marco Polo and John Mandeville. These travellers had visited, in the thirteenth and fourteenth centuries, the remote parts of Asia, far beyond the regions laid down by Ptolemy; and their accounts of the extent of that continent to the eastward had a great effect in convincing Columbus that a voyage to the west, of no long duration, would bring him to its shores, or to the extensive and wealthy islands which lie adjacent. The information concerning Marco Polo is probably derived from Paulo Toscanelli, a celebrated doctor of Florence, already mentioned, with whom Columbus corresponded in 1474, . . .

". . . various indications of land in the west . . . had floated to the shores of the *Reports of Navigators* known world. It is curious to observe, how, when once the mind of Columbus had become heated in the inquiry, it attracted to it every corroborating circumstance, however vague and trivial. He appears to have been particularly attentive to the gleams of information derived from veteran mariners, who had been employed in the recent voyages to the African coasts; and also from the inhabitants of lately discovered islands, placed, in a manner, on the frontier posts of geographical knowledge. All these are carefully noted down among his memorandums, to be collocated with the facts and opinions already stored up in his mind.

"Such, for instance, is the circumstance related to him by Martin Vicenti, a pilot in the service of the King of Portugal; that, after sailing four hundred and fifty leagues to the west of Cape St. Vincent, he had taken from the water a piece of carved wood, which evidently had not been labored with an iron instrument. As the winds had drifted it from the west, it might have come from some unknown land in that direction.

"Pedro Correo, brother-in-law of Columbus, is likewise cited, as having seen, on the island of Porto Santo, a similar piece of wood, which had drifted from the same quarter. He had heard also from the King of Portugal, that reeds of an immense size had floated to some of those islands from the west, in the description of which, Columbus thought he recognized the immense reeds said by Ptolemy to grow in India. . . .

"To these is added the report of a mariner of the port of St. Mary, who asserted that, in the course of a voyage to Ireland, he had seen land to the west, which the ship's company took for some extreme part of Tartary. Other stories, of a similar kind, are noted . . .

"It is singular how much the success of this great undertaking depended upon two happy errors, the imaginary extent of Asia to the east, and the supposed smallness of the earth, both errors of the most learned and profound philosophers, but without which Columbus would hardly have ventured upon his enterprise. . . .

Events in Portugal "Discovery advanced slowly along the coasts of Africa, and the mariners feared to cruise far into the southern hemisphere, with the stars of which they were totally unacquainted. . . .

"The time, however, was at hand, that was to extend the sphere of navigation. The era was propitious to the quick advancement of knowledge. The recent invention of the art of printing enabled men to communicate rapidly and extensively their ideas and discoveries. It drew forth learning from the libraries and convents, and brought it familiarly to the reading-desk of the student. Volumes of information, which before had existed only in costly manuscripts, carefully treasured up, and kept out of the reach of the indigent scholar and obscure artist, were now in every hand. There was henceforth to be no retrogression in knowledge, nor any pause in its career. Every step in advance was immediately, and simultaneously, and widely promulgated, recorded in a thousand forms, and fixed forever. There could never again be a dark age; nations might shut their eyes to the light, and sit in wilfull darkness, but they could not trample it out; it would still shine on, dispensed to happier parts of the world, by the diffusive powers of the press.

"At this juncture, in 1481, a monarch ascended the throne of Portugal, of different ambition from Alphonso. John II., then in the twenty-fifth year of his age, had imbibed the passion for discovery from his grand-uncle Prince Henry, and with his reign all its activity revived. . . .

"The African discoveries had conferred great glory upon Portugal . . . The project of Prince Henry, which had now been tardily prosecuted for half a century, had excited a curiosity about the remote parts of Asia, and revived all the accounts, true and fabulous, of travellers. . . .

". . . John II. partook largely of the popular excitement produced by these narrations. . . . The magnificent idea he had formed of the remote parts of the East made him extremely anxious that the splendid project of Prince Henry should be realized, and the Portuguese flag penetrate to the Indian seas. Impatient of the slowness with which his discoveries advanced along the coast of Africa, and of the impediments which every cape and promontory presented to nautical enterprise, he called in the aid of science to devise some means by which greater scope and certainty might be given to navigation. His two physicians, Roderigo and Joseph ... the most able astronomers and cosmographers of his kingdom, together with the celebrated Martin Behem, entered into a learned consultation on the subject. The result of their conferences and labors was the application of the astrolabe to navigation, enabling the seaman, by the altitude of the sun, to ascertain his distance from the equator. This instrument has since been improved and modified into the modern quadrant, of which, even at its first introduction, it possessed all the essential advantages.

"It is impossible to describe the effect produced upon navigation by this invention. It cast it loose at once from its long bondage to the land, and set it free to rove the deep. The mariner now, instead of coasting the shores like the ancient navigators, and, if driven from the land, groping his way back in doubt and apprehension by the uncertain guidance of the stars, might adventure boldly into unknown seas, confident of being able to trace his course by means of the compass and the astrolabe. ...

"The time when Columbus thus sought his fortunes at the court of Spain coincided with one of the most brilliant periods of the Spanish monarchy. The union of the kingdoms of Arragon and Castile, by the marriage of Ferdinand and Isabella, had consolidated the Christian power in the Peninsula, and put an end to those internal feuds which had so long distracted the country, and insured the domination of the Moslems. The whole force of united Spain was now exerted in the chivalrous enterprise of the Moorish conquest. Under these sovereigns, the various petty kingdoms of Spain began to feel and act as one nation, and to rise to eminence in arts as well as arms. Ferdinand and Isabella ... had

Providential Direction

separate claims to sovereignty, in virtue of their respective kingdoms; they had separate councils, and were often distant from each other in different parts of their empire, each exercising the royal authority. Yet they were so happily united by common views, common interests, and a great deference for each other, that this double administration never prevented a unity of purpose and of action. All acts of sovereignty were executed in both their names; all public writings were subscribed with both their signatures; their likenesses were stamped together on the public coin; and the royal seal displayed the united arms of Castile and Arragon.

"Ferdinand was of the middle stature, well proportioned, and hardy and active from athletic exercise. His carriage was free, erect, and majestic. He had a clear, serene forehead, which appeared more lofty from his head being partly bald. His eyebrows were large and parted, and, like his hair, of a bright chestnut; his eyes were clear and animated; his complexion was somewhat ruddy, and scorched by the toils of war; his mouth moderate, well formed, and gracious in its expression; his teeth white, though small and irregular; his voice sharp; his speech quick and fluent. His genius was clear and comprehensive, his judgment grave and certain. He was simple in dress and diet, equable in his temper, devout in his religion and so indefatigable in business, that it was said he seemed to repose himself by working. He was a great observer and judge of men, and unparalleled in the science of the cabinet. Such is the picture given him by the Spanish historians of his time. It has been added, however, that he had more of bigotry than religion; that his ambition was craving rather than magnanimous; that he made war less like a paladin than a prince, less for glory than for mere dominion; and that his policy was cold, selfish, and artful. He was called the wise and prudent in Spain; in Italy, the pious; in

FERDINAND AND ISABELLA.

France and England, the ambitious and perfidious. He certainly was one of the most subtle statesmen, but one of the most thorough egotists that ever sat upon a throne. . . .

"Contemporary writers have been enthusiastic in their descriptions of Isabella, but time has sanctioned their eulogies. She is one of the purest and most beautiful characters in the pages of history. She was well formed, of the middle size, with great dignity and gracefulness of deportment, and a mingled gravity and sweetness of demeanor. Her complexion was fair; her hair auburn, inclining to red; her eyes were of a clear blue, with a benign expression, and there was a singular modesty in her countenance, gracing, as it did, a wonderful firmness of purpose and earnestness of spirit. Though strongly attached to her husband and studious of his fame, yet she always maintained her distinct rights as an allied prince. She exceeded him in beauty, in personal dignity, in acuteness of genius, and in grandeur of soul. Combining the active and resolute qualities of man with the softer charities of woman, she mingled in the warlike councils of her husband, engaged personally in his enterprises, and in some instances surpassed him in the firmness and intrepidity of her measures; while, being inspired with a truer idea of glory, she infused a more lofty and generous temper into his subtle and calculating policy.

"It is in the civil history of their reign, however, that the character of Isabella shines most illustrious. Her fostering and maternal care was continually directed to reform the laws, and heal the ills engendered by a long course of internal wars. She loved her people, and while diligently seeking their good, she mitigated, as much as possible, the harsh measures of her husband, directed to the same end, but inflamed by a mistaken zeal. . . . While all her public thoughts and acts were princely and august, her private habits were simple, frugal, and unostentatious. In the intervals of state business she assembled round her the ablest men in literature and science, and directed herself by their counsels, in promoting letters and arts. Through her patronage, Salamanca rose to that height which it assumed among the learned institutions of the age. She promoted the distribution of honors and rewards for the promulgation of knowledge; she fostered the art of printing recently invented, and encouraged the establishment of presses in every part of the kingdom; books were admitted free of all duty, and more, we are told, were printed in Spain, at that early period of the art, than in the present literary age.

"It is wonderful how much the destinies of countries depend at times upon the virtues of individuals, and how it is given to great spirits by combining, exciting, and directing the latent powers of a nation, to stamp it, as it were, with their own greatness. Such beings realize the idea of guardian angels, appointed by Heaven to watch over the destinies of empires. Such had been Prince Henry for the kingdom of Portugal; and such was now for Spain the illustrious Isabella. . . .

"Wherever he [Columbus] obtained a candid hearing from intelligent auditors, the dignity of his manners, his earnest sincerity, the elevation of his views, and the practical shrewdness of his demonstrations, commanded respect even where they failed to produce conviction. . . . *Columbus's Character*

"In the winter Columbus followed the court to Salamanca. Here his zealous friend, Alonzo de Quintanilla, exerted his influence to obtain for him the countenance of the celebrated Pedro Gonzalez de Mendoza, Archbishop of Toledo, and Grand Cardinal of Spain. This was the most important personage about the court; and was facetiously called by Peter Martyr the 'third king of Spain.' . . . He was pleased with the noble and earnest manner of Columbus, which showed him to be no common schemer; he felt the grandeur, and, at the same time, the simplicity of his theory, and the force of many of the arguments by which it was supported. He determined that it was a matter highly worthy of the consideration of the sovereigns, and through his representations Columbus at length obtained admission to the royal presence.

". . . Columbus appeared in the royal presence with modesty, yet self-possession, neither dazzled nor daunted by the splendor of the court or the awful majesty of the throne. He unfolded his plan with eloquence and zeal, for he felt himself, as he afterward declared, kindled as with a fire from on high, and considered himself the agent chosen by Heaven to accomplish its grand designs.

"Ferdinand was too keen a judge of men not to appreciate the character of Columbus. He perceived that, however soaring might be his imagination, and vast and visionary his views, his whole scheme had scientific and practical foundation. . . .

Council at Salamanca "What a striking spectacle must the hall of the old convent have presented at this memorable conference! A simple mariner, standing forth in the midst of an imposing array of professors, friars, and dignitaries of the church; maintaining his theory with natural eloquence, and, as it were, pleading the cause of the new world. . . .

"When Columbus took his stand before this learned body, he had appeared the plain and simple navigator; somewhat daunted, perhaps, by the greatness of his task and the august nature of his auditory. But he had a degree of religious feeling which gave him a confidence in the execution of what he conceived his great errand, and he was of an ardent temperament that became heated in action by its own generous fires. . . . casting aside his maps and charts, and discarding for a time his practical and scientific lore, his visionary spirit took fire at the doctrinal objections of his opponents, and he met them upon their own ground, pouring forth those magnificent texts of Scripture, and those mysterious predictions of the prophets, which, in his enthusiastic moments, he considered as types and annunciations of the sublime discovery which he proposed!"

Columbus welcomed the termination of Spain's campaign against the Moors, hoping to at last receive a decision about his proposed enterprise. But he was again disappointed.

"If the bustle and turmoil of this campaign prevented the intended conference, the concerns of Columbus fared no better during the subsequent rejoicings. Ferdinand and Isabella entered Seville in February, 1490, with great pomp and triumph. There were then preparations made for the marriage of their eldest daughter, the Princess Isabella, with the Prince Don Alonzo, heir apparent of Portugal. . . . Throughout the whole winter and spring the court was in a continual tumult of parade and pleasure, and nothing was to be seen at Seville but feasts, tournaments, and torchlight processions. What chance had Columbus of being heard amid these alternate uproars of war and festivity? . . .

"During all this time he was exposed to continual scoffs and indignities, being ridiculed by the light and ignorant as a mere dreamer, and stigmatized by the illiberal as an adventurer. The very children, it is said, pointed to their foreheads as he passed, being taught to regard him as a kind of madman.

"The summer of 1490 passed away, but still Columbus was kept in tantalizing and tormenting suspense. The subsequent winter was not more propitious. He was lingering at Cordova in a state of irritating anxiety, when he learnt that the sovereigns were preparing to depart on a campaign in the Vega of Granada, with a determination never to raise their camp from before that city until their victorious banners should float upon its towers.

"Columbus was aware that when once the campaign was opened and the sovereigns were in the field, it would be in vain to expect any attention to his suit. He was wearied, if not incensed, at the repeated postponements he had experienced by which several years had been consumed. . . . Renouncing all further confidence, therefore, in vague promises, which had so often led to disappointment, and giving up all hopes of countenance from the throne, he turned his back upon Seville, indignant at the thoughts of having been beguiled out of so many precious years of waning existence.

"About half a league from the little seaport of Palos de Moguer in Andalusia there *Providential Encouragement* stood . . . an ancient convent of Franciscan friars dedicated to Santa Maria de Rabida. One day a stranger on foot, in humble guise but of a distinguished air, accompanied by a small boy, stopped at the gate of the convent and asked of the porter a little bread and water for his child. While receiving this humble refreshment, the prior of the convent, Juan Perez de Marchena, happening to pass by, was struck with the appearance of the stranger, and observing from his air and accent that he was a foreigner, entered into conversation with him, and soon learned the particulars of his story. That stranger was Columbus.

"The prior was a man of extensive information. His attention had been turned in some measure to geographical and nautical science, probably from his vicinity to Palos, the inhabitants of which were among the most enterprising navigators of Spain, and made frequent voyages to the recently discovered islands and countries on the African coast. He was greatly interested by the conversation of Columbus, and struck with the grandeur of his views. . . .

"When he found, however, that the voyager was on the point of abandoning Spain to seek patronage in the court of France and that so important an enterprise was about to be lost forever to the country, the patriotism of the good friar took alarm. He detained Columbus as his guest, and, diffident of his own judgment, sent for a scientific friend to converse with him. That friend was Garcia Fernandez, a physician resident in Palos . . . Fernandez was equally struck with the appearance and conversation of the stranger; several conferences took place at the convent, at which several of the veteran mariners of Palos were present. Among these was Martin Alonzo Pinzon, the head of a family of wealthy and experienced navigators of the place, celebrated for their adventurous expeditions. . . .

"Friar Juan Perez was confirmed in his faith by the concurrence of those learned and practical councillors. He had once been confessor to the queen, and knew she was always accessible to persons of his sacred calling. He proposed to write to her immediately on the subject, and entreated Columbus to delay his journey until an answer could be received. The latter was easily persuaded, for he felt as if, in leaving Spain, he was again abandoning his home. He was also reluctant to renew, in another court, the vexations and disappointments experienced in Spain and Portugal.

"The little council at the convent of La Rabida now cast round their eyes for an ambassador to depart upon this momentous mission. They chose one Sebastian Rodriguez . . . The honest pilot acquitted himself faithfully, expeditiously, and successfully in his embassy. He found access to the benignant princess, and delivered the epistle of the friar. Isabella had always been favorably disposed to the proposition of Columbus. She wrote in reply to Juan Perez, thanking him for his timely services, and requesting that he would repair immediately to the court, leaving Christopher Columbus in confident hope until he should hear further from her. . . .

"The sacred office of Juan Perez gained him a ready entrance in a court distinguished for religious zeal . . . He pleaded the cause of Columbus with characteristic enthusiasm, speaking from actual knowledge of his honorable motives, his professional knowledge and experience, and his perfect capacity to fulfill the undertaking; he represented the solid principles upon which the enterprise was founded, the advantage that must attend its success, and the glory it must shed upon the Spanish crown. . . . The queen requested that Columbus might be again sent to her, and, with the kind considerateness which characterized her, bethinking herself of his poverty, and his humble plight, ordered that twenty thousand maravedies in florins should be forwarded to him, to bear his travelling expenses, to provide him with a mule for his journey, and to furnish him with decent raiment, that he might make a respectable appearance at the court. . . .

"It is impossible not to admire the great constancy of purpose and loftiness of spirit displayed by Columbus, ever since he had conceived the sublime idea of his discovery. More than eighteen years had elapsed since his correspondence with Paulo Toscanelli of Florence, wherein he had announced his design. The greatest part of that time had been consumed in applications at various courts. During that period, what poverty, neglect, ridicule, contumely, and disappointment had he not suffered! Nothing, however, could shake his perseverance, nor make him descend to terms which he considered beneath the dignity of his enterprise. In all his negotiations he forgot his present obscurity; he forgot his present indigence; his ardent imagination realized the magnitude of his contemplated discoveries, and he felt himself negotiating about empire. . . .

Queen Isabella

". . . With an enthusiasm worthy of herself and of the cause, Isabella exclaimed 'I undertake the enterprise for my own crown of Castile, and will pledge my jewels to raise the necessary funds.' This was the proudest moment in the life of Isabella; it stamped her renown forever as the patroness of the discovery of the New World. . . ."

Terms of Agreement

1. "That Columbus should have, for himself during his life, and his heirs and successors forever, the office of admiral in all the lands and continents which he might discover or acquire in the ocean, with similar honors and prerogatives to those enjoyed by the high admiral of Castile in his district.
2. "That he should be viceroy and governor-general over all the said lands and continents, with the privilege of nominating three candidates for the government of each island or province, one of whom should be selected by the sovereigns.
3. "That he should be entitled to reserve for himself one tenth of all pearls, precious stones, gold, silver, spices, and all other articles and merchandises, in whatever manner found, bought, bartered, or gained within his admiralty, the costs being first deducted.
4. "That he, or his lieutenant, should be the sole judge in all causes and disputes arising out of traffic between those countries and Spain provided the high admiral of Castile had similar jurisdiction in his district.
5. "That he might then, and at all after times, contribute an eighth part of the expense in fitting out vessels to sail on this enterprise, and receive an eighth part of the profits. . . .

Furnishing Ships

". . . a royal order was read by a notary public, commanding the authorities of Palos to have two cara-vels ready for sea within ten days . . . and to place them and their crews at the disposal of Columbus. . . .

"With these orders the authorities promised implicit compliance; but when the nature of the intended expedition came to be known, astonishment and dismay fell upon the little community. The ships and crews demanded for such a desperate service were regarded in the light of sacrifices. The owners of vessels refused to furnish them; the boldest seamen shrank from such a wild and chimerical cruise into the wilderness of the ocean. . . .

"Weeks elapsed without a vessel being procured, or anything else being done in fulfilment of the royal orders. . . . The communities of those places were thrown into complete confusion; tumults took place; but nothing of consequence was effected. At length Martin Alonzo Pinzon stepped forward, with his brother Vicente Yañez Pinzon, both navigators of great courage and ability, owners of vessels, and having seamen in their employ. . . . They engaged to sail on the expedition, and furnished one of the vessels required. Others, with their owners and crews, were pressed into the service by the magistrates under the arbitrary mandate of the sovereigns; and it is a striking instance of the despotic authority exercised over commerce in those times, that respectable individuals should thus be compelled to engage, with persons and ships, in what appeared to them a mad and desperate enterprise. During the equipment of the vessels, troubles and difficulties arose among the seamen who had been compelled to embark. . . . All kinds of obstacles were thrown in the way . . . to retard or defeat the voyage. The calkers employed upon the vessels did their work in a careless and imperfect manner, and on being commanded to do it over again absconded. Some of the seamen who had enlisted willingly repented of their hardihood, or were dissuaded by their relatives, and sought to retract; others deserted and concealed themselves. Everything had to be effected by the most harsh and arbitrary measures, and in defiance of popular prejudice and opposition.

"The influence and example of the Pinzons had a great effect in allaying this opposition, and inducing many of their friends and relatives to embark. It is supposed that they had furnished Columbus with funds to pay the eighth part of the expense which he was bound to advance. It is also said that Martin Alonzo Pinzon was to divide with him his share of the profits. . . . It is certain . . . that the assistance of the Pinzons was all-important, if not indispensable, in fitting out and launching the expedition.

"After the great difficulties made by various courts in patronizing this enterprise, it is surprising how inconsiderable armament was required. It is evident that Columbus had reduced his requisitions to the narrowest limits . . . The smallness of the vessels was considered an advantage by Columbus, in a voyage of discovery, enabling him to run close to the shores, and to enter shallow rivers and harbors. . . . But that such long and perilous expeditions, into unknown seas, should be undertaken in vessels without decks, and that they should live through the violent tempests, by which they were frequently assailed, remain among the singular circumstances of these daring voyages. . . .

THE THREE CARAVELS.

Importance of Recording

"When Columbus set sail on this memorable voyage, he commenced a regular journal, intended for the inspection of the Spanish sovereigns. Like all his other transactions, it evinces how deeply he was impressed with the grandeur and solemnity of his enterprise. He proposed to keep it, as he afterward observed, in the manner of the Commentaries of Caesar. It opened with a stately prologue, wherein, in the following words, were set forth the motives and views which led to his expedition.

"'In nomine D. N. Jesu Christi. Whereas most Christian, most high, most excellent and most powerful princes, king and queen of the Spains, and of the islands of the sea, our sovereigns, in the present year of 1492, after your highnesses had put an end to the war with the Moors who ruled in Europe . . . I departed . . . from the city of Granada, on Saturday, the 12th of May, of the same year 1492, to Palos, a seaport, where I armed three ships, well calculated for such service, and sailed from that port well furnished with provisions and with many seamen, on Friday, the third of August, of the same year, half an hour before sunrise, and took the route for the Canary Islands of your highnesses to steer my course thence, and navigate until I should arrive at the Indies . . . For this purpose I intend to write during this voyage, very punctually from day to day, all that I may do, and see, and experience, as will hereafter be seen. Also, my sovereign princes, besides describing each night all that has occurred in the day, and in the day the navigation of the night, I propose to make a chart in which I will set down the waters and lands of the Ocean sea in their proper situations under their bearings; and further, to compose a book, and illustrate the whole in picture . . . and upon the whole it will be essential that I should forget sleep and attend closely to the navigation to accomplish these things, which will be a great labor.' . . .

"It was on Friday, the 3d of August, 1492, early in the morning, that Columbus set sail . . . steering in a *Providential Beginnings* south-westerly direction for the Canary Islands, whence it was his intention to strike due west. As a guide by which to sail, he had prepared a map or chart, improved upon that sent him by Paulo Toscanelli. Neither of these now exist, but the globe or planisphere finished by Martin Behem in this year of the admiral's first voyage is still extant, and furnishes an idea of what the chart of Columbus must have been. It exhibits the coasts of Europe and Africa from the south of Ireland to the end of Guinea, and opposite to them, on the other side of the Atlantic, the extremity of Asia, or, as it was termed, India. Between them is placed the island of Cipango, or Japan, which, according to Marco Polo, lay fifteen hundred miles distant from the Asiatic coast. In his computations Columbus advanced this island about a thousand leagues too much to the east, supposing it to be about the situation of Florida; and at this island he hoped first to arrive.

"The exultation of Columbus at finding himself, after so many years of baffled hope, fairly launched on his grand enterprise, was checked by his want of confidence in the resolution and perseverance of his crews. As long as he remained within reach of Europe, there was no security that, in a moment of repentance and alarm, they might not renounce the prosecution of the voyage, and insist on a return. Symptoms soon appeared to warrant his apprehensions. On the third day the Pinta made signal of distress; her rudder was discovered to be broken and unhung. This Columbus surmised to be done through the contrivance of the owners of the caravel, Gomez Rascon and Christoval Quintero, to disable their vessel, and cause her to be left behind. As has already been observed, they had been pressed into the service greatly against their will, and their caravel seized upon for the expedition, in conformity to the royal orders.

"Columbus was much disturbed at this occurrence. It gave him a foretaste of further difficulties to be apprehended from crews partly enlisted on compulsion, and all full of doubt and foreboding. Trivial obstacles might, in the present critical state of his voyage, spread panic and mutiny through his ships, and entirely defeat the expedition.

"The wind was blowing strongly at the time, so that he could not render assistance without endangering his own vessel. Fortunately, Martin Alonzo Pinzon commanded the Pinta, and being an adroit and able seaman, succeeded in securing the rudder with cords, so as to bring the vessel into management. This, however, was but a temporary and inadequate expedient; the fastenings gave way again on the following day, and the other ships were obliged to shorten sail until the rudder could be secured.

GOOD-BY, COLUMBUS!

"This damaged state of the Pinta, as well as her being in a leaky condition, determined the admiral to touch at the Canary Islands, and seek a vessel to replace her.

"They were detained upward of three weeks among these islands, seeking in vain another vessel. They were obliged, therefore, to make a new rudder for the Pinta, and repair her for the voyage. The latine sails of the Nina were also altered into square sails, that she might work more steadily and securely, and be able to keep company with the other vessels.

"While sailing among these islands, the crew were terrified at beholding the lofty peak of Teneriffe sending forth volumes of flame and smoke, being ready to take alarm at any extraordinary phenomenon, and to construe it into a disastrous portent. Columbus took great pains to dispel their apprehensions, explaining the natural causes of those volcanic fires, and verifying his explanations by citing Mount Etna and other well-known volcanoes.

"While taking in wood and water and provisions in the island of Gomera, a vessel arrived from Ferro, which reported that three Portuguese caravels had been seen hovering off that island, with the intention, it was said, of capturing Columbus. The admiral suspected some hostile stratagem on the part of the King of Portugal, in revenge for his having embarked in the service of Spain; he therefore lost no time in putting to sea, anxious to get far from those islands, and out of the track of navigation, trembling lest something might occur to defeat his expedition, commenced under such inauspicious circumstances.

Man Proposes,
God Disposes

"Early in the morning of the 6th of September Columbus set sail from the island of Gomera, and now might be said first to strike into the region of discovery; taking leave of these frontier islands of the Old World, and steering westward for the unknown parts of the Atlantic. For three days, however, a profound calm kept the vessels loitering with flagging sails within a short distance of the land. . . .

"On losing sight of this last trace of land, the hearts of the crews failed them. They seemed literally to have taken leave of the world. Behind them was everything dear to the heart of man; country, family, friends, life itself; before them everything was chaos, mystery, and peril. In the perturbation of the moment, they despaired of ever more seeing their homes. Many of the rugged seamen shed tears, and some broke into loud lamentations. The admiral tried in every way to soothe their distress, and to inspire them with his own glorious anticipations. He described to them the magnificent countries to which he was about to conduct them: the islands of the Indian seas teeming with gold and precious stones; the regions of Mangi and Cathay, with their cities of unrivalled wealth and splendor. He promised them land and riches, and everything that could arouse their cupidity or inflame their imaginations, nor were these promises made for purposes of mere deception; he certainly believed that he should realize them all. . . .

"On the 13th of September . . . Columbus for the first time noticed the variation of the needle . . . He perceived about nightfall that the needle, instead of pointing to the north star, varied about half a point, or between five and six degrees, to the north-

Fixed
Principles of
Universe

west, and still more on the following morning. Struck with this circumstance, he observed it attentively for days, and found that the variation increased as he advanced. He at first made no mention of this phenomenon, knowing how ready his people were to take alarm, but it soon attracted the attention of the pilots, and filled them with consternation. . . .

"Columbus tasked his science and ingenuity for reasons with which to allay their terror. He observed that the direction of the needle was not to the polar star, but to some fixed and invisible point. The variation, therefore, was not caused by any fallacy in the compass, but by the movement of the north star itself, which, like the other heavenly bodies, had its changes and revolutions, and every day described a circle round the pole. The high opinion which the pilots entertained of Columbus as a profound astronomer, gave weight to this theory, and their alarm subsided. As yet the solar system of Copernicus was unknown; the explanation of Columbus, therefore was highly plausible and ingenious, and it shows the vivacity of his mind, ever ready to meet the emergency of the moment. . . .

"On the 14th of September the voyagers were rejoiced by the sight of what they considered harbingers of

Difficult
Days

land. A heron, and a tropical bird . . . neither of which is supposed to venture far to sea, hovered about the ships. . . .

"They now began to see large patches of herbs and weeds drifting from the west, and increasing in quantity as they advanced. Some of these weeds were such as grow about rocks, others such as are produced in rivers; some were yellow and withered, others so green as to have apparently been recently washed from land. On one of these patches was a live crab, which Columbus carefully preserved. They saw also a white tropical bird, of a kind which never sleeps upon the sea. . . .

"The crews were all in high spirits; each ship strove to get in the advance, and every seaman was eagerly on the look-out; for the sovereigns had promised a pension of ten thousand maravedis to him who should first discover land. Martin Alonzo Pinzon crowded all canvas, and, as the Pinta was a fast sailer, he generally kept the lead. In the afternoon he hailed the admiral and informed him that, from the flight of a great number of birds and from the appearance of the northern horizon, he thought there was land in that direction.

"There was in fact a cloudiness in the north, such as often hangs over land; and at sunset it assumed such shapes and masses that many fancied they beheld islands. There was a universal wish, therefore, to steer for that quarter. Columbus, however, was persuaded that they were mere illusions. Every one who has made a sea voyage must have witnessed the deceptions caused by clouds resting upon the horizon, especially about sunset and sunrise; which the eye, assisted by the imagination and desire, easily converts into the wished-for land. This is particularly the case within the tropics, where the clouds at sunset assume the most singular appearances. . . .

"Notwithstanding his precaution to keep the people ignorant of the distance they had sailed, they were now growing extremely uneasy at the length of the voyage. They had advanced much farther west than ever man had sailed before, and though already beyond the reach of succor, still they continued daily leaving vast tracts of ocean behind them, and pressing onward and onward into that apparently boundless abyss. It is true they had been flattered by various indications of land, and still others were occurring; but all mocked them with vain hopes: after being hailed with a transient joy, they passed away, one after another, and the same interminable expanse of sea and sky continued to extend before them. Even the bland and gentle breeze, uniformly aft, was now conjured by their ingenious fears into a cause of alarm; for they began to imagine that the wind, in these seas, might always prevail from the east, and if so, would never permit their return to Spain.

"Columbus endeavored to dispel these gloomy presages sometimes by argument and expostulation, sometimes by awakening fresh hopes, and pointing out new signs of land. On the 20th of September the wind veered, with light breezes from the south-west. These, though adverse to their progress, had a cheering effect upon the people, as they proved that the wind did not always prevail from the east. Several birds also visited the ships; three, of a small kind which keep about groves and orchards, came singing in the morning, and flew away again in the evening. Their song cheered the hearts of the dismayed mariners, who hailed it as the voice of land. The larger fowl, they observed, were strong of wing, and might venture far to sea; but such small birds were too feeble to fly far, and their singing showed that they were not exhausted by their flight.

"On the following day there was either a profound calm or light winds from the south-west. The sea, as far as the eye could reach, was covered with weeds; a phenomenon, often observed in this part of the ocean, which has sometimes the appearance of a vast inundated meadow. . . . These fields of weeds were at first regarded with great satisfaction, but at length they became, in many places, so dense and matted as in some degree to impede the sailing of the ships, which must have been under very little headway. The crews now called to mind some tale about the frozen ocean, where ships were said to be sometimes fixed immovable. They endeavored, therefore, to avoid as much as possible these floating masses, lest some disaster of the kind might happen to themselves. Others considered these weeds as proof that the sea was growing shallower, and began to talk of lurking rocks, and shoals, and treacherous quicksands; and of the danger of running aground, as it were, in the midst of the ocean, where their vessels might rot and fall to pieces, far out of the track of human aid, and without any shore where the crews might take refuge. . . .

"To dispel these fears, the admiral had frequent recourse to the lead; but though he sounded with a deep-sea line, he still found no bottom. The minds of the crews, however, had gradually become diseased. They were full of vague terrors and superstitious fancies: they construed everything into a cause of alarm, and harassed their commander by incessant murmurs. . . .

"Columbus continued with admirable patience to reason with these fancies; . . .Terror, however, multiplies and varies the forms of ideal danger a thousand times faster than the most active wisdom can dispel them. The more Columbus argued, the more boisterous became the murmurs of his crew, until, on Sunday, the 25th of September, there came on a heavy swell of the sea, unaccompanied by wind. . . .

"Columbus, who as usual considered himself under the immediate eye and guardianship of Heaven in this solemn enterprise, intimates in his journal that this swelling of the sea seemed providentially ordered to allay the rising clamors of his crew; comparing it to that which so miraculously aided Moses when conducting the children of Israel out of the captivity of Egypt.

"The situation of Columbus was daily becoming more and more critical. In proportion as he approached the regions where he expected to find land, the impatience of his crews augmented. The favorable signs which increased his confidence, were derided by them as delusive; and there was danger of their rebelling, and obliging him to turn back, when on the point of realizing the object of all his labors. . . .

"In this way they fed each other's discontents, gathering together in little knots, and fomenting a spirit of mutinous opposition; and when we consider . . . that a great part of these men were sailing on compulsion, we cannot wonder that there was imminent danger of their breaking forth into open rebellion and compelling Columbus to turn back. . . .

"Columbus was not ignorant of the mutinous disposition of his crew, but he still maintained a serene and steady countenance; soothing some with gentle words; endeavoring to stimulate the pride or avarice of others, and openly menacing the refractory with signal punishment, should they do anything to impede the voyage.

"On the 25th of September the wind again became favorable, and they were able to resume their course directly to the west. The airs being light and the sea calm, the vessels sailed near to each other, and Columbus had much conversation with Martin Alonzo Pinzon on the subject of a chart which the former had sent three days before on board of the Pinta. Pinzon thought that, according to the indications of the map, they ought to be in the neighborhood of Cipango, and the other islands which the admiral had therein delineated. Columbus partly entertained the same idea, but thought it possible that the ships might have been borne out of their track by the prevalent currents, or that they had not come so far as the pilots had reckoned. He desired that the chart might be returned, and Pinzon, tying it to the end of a cord, flung it on board to him. While Columbus, his pilot, and several of his experienced mariners were studying the map, and endeavoring to make out from it their actual position, they heard a shout from the Pinta, and looking up, beheld Martin Alonzo Pinzon mounted on the stern of his vessel crying 'Land! land! Senor I claim my reward!' He pointed at the same time to the south-west, where there was indeed an appearance of land at about twenty-five leagues' distance. Upon this Columbus threw himself on his knees and returned thanks to God; and Martin Alonzo repeated the *Gloria in excelsis,* in which he was joined by his own crew and that of the admiral.

". . . The morning light, however, put an end to all their hopes, as to a dream. The fancied land proved to be nothing but an evening cloud, and had vanished in the night. With dejected hearts they once more resumed their western course . . .

"For several days they continued on with the same propitious breeze, tranquil sea, and mild, delightful weather. The water was so calm that the sailors amused themselves with swimming about the vessel. Dolphins began to abound, and flying fish, darting into the air, fell upon the decks. The continued signs of land diverted the attention of the crews, and insensibly beguiled them onward.

"On the 1st of October, according to the reckoning of the pilot of the admiral's ship, they had come five hundred and eighty leagues west of the Canary Islands. . . . On the following day the weeds floated from east to west; and on the third day no birds were to be seen.

"The crews now began to fear that they had passed between islands, from one to the other of which the birds had been flying. Columbus had also some doubts of the kind, but refused to alter his westward course. The people again uttered murmurs and menaces; but on the following day they were visited by such flights of birds, and the various indications of land became so numerous, that from a state of despondency they passed to one of confident expectation.

"Eager to obtain the promised pension, the seamen were continually giving the cry of land, on the least appearance of the kind. To put a stop to these false alarms, which produced continual disappointments, Columbus declared that should any one give such notice, and land not be discovered within three days afterward, he should thenceforth forfeit all claim to the reward.

"On the evening of the 6th of October, Martin Alonzo Pinzon began to lose confidence in their present course, and proposed that they should stand more to the southward. Columbus, however, still persisted in steering directly west. . . .

"On the morning of the 7th of October, at sunrise, several of the admiral's crew thought they beheld land in the west, but so indistinctly that no one ventured to proclaim it . . . As they advanced, however, their cloud-built hopes faded away, and before evening the fancied land had again melted into the air.

"The crews now sank into a degree of dejection proportioned to their recent excitement; but new circumstances occurred to arouse them. Columbus, having observed great flights of small field-birds going toward the south-west, concluded they must be secure of some neighboring land, where they would find food and a resting-place. He knew the importance which the Portuguese voyagers attached to the flight of birds, by following which they had discovered most of their islands. He had now come seven hundred and fifty leagues, the distance at which he had computed to find the island of Cipango; as there was no appearance of it, he might have

missed it through some mistake in the latitude. He determined, therefore, on the evening of the 7th of October, to alter his course to the west-south-west, the direction in which the birds generally flew, and continue that direction for at least two days. . . .

"For three days they stood in this direction, and the further they went the more frequent and encouraging were the signs of land. Flights of small birds of various colors, some of them such as sing in the fields, came flying about the ships, and they continued toward the south-west . . . a heron, a pelican, and a duck were seen, all bound in the same direction. The herbage which floated by was fresh and green, as if recently from land, and the air, Columbus observes, was sweet and fragrant as April breezes in Seville.

"All these, however, were regarded by the crews as so many delusions beguiling them on to destruction; and when on the evening of the third day they beheld the sun go down upon a shoreless ocean, they broke forth into turbulent clamor. They exclaimed against this obstinacy in tempting fate by continuing on into a boundless sea. They insisted upon turning homeward, and abandoning the voyage as hopeless. Columbus endeavored to pacify them by gentle words and promises of large rewards; but finding that they only increased in clamor, he assumed a decided tone. He told them it was useless to murmur, the expedition had been sent by the sovereigns to seek the Indies, and, happen what might he was determined to persevere, until, by the blessing of God, he should accomplish the enterprise.

"Columbus was now at open defiance with his crew, and his situation became desperate. Fortunately the manifestations of the vicinity to land were such on the following day as no longer to admit a doubt. Besides a quantity of fresh weeds, such as grow in rivers, they saw a green fish of a kind which keeps about rocks; then a branch of thorn with berries on it, and recently separated from the tree, floated by them; then they picked up a reed, a small board, and, above all, a staff artificially carved. All gloom and mutiny now gave way to sanguine expectation; and throughout the day each one was eagerly on the watch, in hopes of being the first to discover the long-sought-for land.

"In the evening, when, according to invariable custom on board of the admiral's ship, the mariners had sung the . . . vesper hymn to the Virgin, he made an impressive address to his crew. He pointed out the goodness of God in thus conducting them by soft and favoring breezes across a tranquil ocean, cheering their hopes continually with fresh signs, increasing as their fears augmented, and thus leading and guiding them to a promised land. He thought it probable they would make land that very night; he ordered, therefore, a vigilant look-out to be kept from the forecastle, promising to whomsoever should make the discovery, a doublet of velvet, in addition to the pension to be given by the sovereigns.

". . . As the evening darkened, Columbus took his station on the top of the castle or cabin on the high poop of his vessel, ranging his eye along the dusky horizon, and maintaining an intense and unremitting watch. About ten o'clock he thought he beheld a light glimmering at a great distance. Fearing his eager hopes might deceive him, he called to Pedro Gutierrez, gentleman of the king's bedchamber, and inquired whether he saw such a light; the latter replied in the affirmative. Doubtful whether it might not yet be some delusion of the fancy, Columbus called Rodrigo Sanchez of Segovia, and made the same inquiry. By the time the latter had ascended the round-house the light had disappeared. They saw it once or twice afterward in sudden and passing gleams; as if it were a torch in the bark of a fisherman, rising and sinking with the waves; or in the hand of some person on shore, borne up and down as he walked from house to house. . . .

"They continued their course until two in the morning, when a gun from the Pinta gave the joyful signal of land. It was first descried by a mariner named Rodrigo de Triana; but the reward was afterward adjudged to the admiral, for having previously perceived the light. The land was now clearly seen about two leagues distant, whereupon they took in sail and lay to, waiting impatiently for the dawn.

"The thoughts and feelings of Columbus in this little space of time must have been tumultuous and intense. At length, in spite of every difficulty and danger, he had accomplished his object. The great mystery of the ocean was revealed; his theory, which had been the scoff of sages, was triumphantly established; he had secured to himself a glory durable as the world itself.

"It is difficult to conceive the feelings of such a man, at such a moment; or the conjectures which must have thronged upon his mind, as to the land before him, covered with darkness. . . .

"It was on Friday morning, the 12th of October, that Columbus first beheld the New World. As the day *Vision Achieved* dawned he saw before him a level island, several leagues in extent, and covered with trees like a continual orchard. Though apparently uncultivated, it was populous, for the inhabitants were seen issuing from all parts of the woods and running to the shore. They were perfectly naked, and, as they stood gazing at the ships, appeared by their attitudes and gestures to be lost in astonishment. Columbus made signal for the ships to cast anchor, and the boats to be manned and armed. He entered his own boat, richly attired in scarlet, and holding the royal standard; while Martin Alonzo Pinzon and Vincent Yañez his brother, put off in company in their boats, each with a banner of the enterprise emblazoned with a green cross, having on either side the letters F. and Y., the initials of the Castilian monarchs Fernando and Ysabel, surmounted by crowns.

". . . On landing he threw himself on his knees, kissed the earth, and returned thanks to God with tears of joy. His example was followed by the rest, whose hearts indeed overflowed with the same feelings of gratitude. Columbus then rising drew his sword, displayed the royal standard, and assembling round him the two captains . . . he took solemn possession in the name of the Castilian sovereigns, giving the island the name of San Salvador. . . .

"The feelings of the crew now burst forth in the most extravagant transports. They had

96

recently considered themselves devoted men, hurrying forward to destruction; they now looked upon themselves as favorites of fortune, and gave themselves up to the most unbounded joy. They thronged around the admiral with overflowing zeal, some embracing him, others kissing his hands. Those who had been most mutinous and turbulent during the voyage, were now most devoted and enthusiastic. Some begged favors of him, as if he had already wealth and honors in his gift. Many abject spirits who had outraged him by their insolence, now crouched at his feet, begging pardon for all the trouble they had caused him, and promising the blindest obedience for the future. . . .

"As Columbus supposed himself to have landed on an island at the extremity of India, he called the natives by the general appellation of Indians, which was universally adopted before the true nature of his discovery was known, and has since been extended to all the aboriginals of the New World.

"The islanders were friendly and gentle. Their only arms were lances, hardened at the end by fire, or pointed with a flint, or the teeth or bone of a fish. There was not iron to be seen, nor did they appear acquainted with its properties; for, when a drawn sword was presented to them, they unguardedly took it by the edge. . . .

"The avarice of the discoverers was quickly excited by the sight of small ornaments of gold, worn by some of the natives in their noses. These the latter gladly exchanged for glass beads and hawks' bells; and both parties exulted in the bargain, no doubt admiring each other's simplicity. As gold, however, was an object of royal monopoly in all enterprises of discovery, Columbus forbade any traffic in it without his express sanction; and he put the same prohibition on the traffic for cotton, reserving to the crown all trade for it, wherever it should be found in any quantity.

"He inquired of the natives where this gold was procured. They answered him by signs, pointing to the south, where, he understood them, dwelt a king of such wealth that he was served in vessels of wrought gold. . . . He was persuaded that he had arrived among the islands described by Marco Polo as lying opposite to Cathay, in the Chinese sea, and he construed everything to accord with the account given of those opulent regions. . . . The country to the south, abounding in gold, could be no other than the famous island of Cipango; and the king who was served out of vessels of gold must be the monarch whose magnificent city and gorgeous palace, covered with plates of gold, had been extolled in such splendid terms by Marco Polo. . . .

"On the 19th [of November] Columbus again put to sea, and for two days made ineffectual *The Lord's Direction* attempts, against head winds, to reach an island directly east, about sixty miles distant, which he supposed to be Babeque. The wind continuing obstinately adverse and the sea rough, he put his ship about toward evening of the 20th, making signals for the other vessels to follow him. His signals were unattended by the Pinta, which was considerably to the eastward. Columbus repeated the signals, but they were still unattended to. Night coming on, he shortened sail and hoisted signal lights to the masthead, thinking Pinzon would yet join him, which he could easily do, having the wind astern; but when the morning dawned the Pinta was no longer to be seen.

"Columbus was disquieted by this circumstance. Pinzon was a veteran navigator, accustomed to hold a high rank among his nautical associates. The squadron had in a great measure been manned and fitted out through his influence and exertions; he could ill brook subordination therefore to Columbus, whom he perhaps did not consider his superior in skill and knowledge, and who had been benefited by his purse. Several misunderstandings and disputes had accordingly occurred between them in the course of the voyage, and when Columbus saw Pinzon thus parting company, without any appointed rendezvous, he suspected either that he intended to take upon himself a separate command and prosecute the enterprise in his own name, or hasten back to Spain and bear off the glory of the discovery. To attempt to seek him, however, was fruitless: he was far out of sight; his vessel was a superior sailer, and it was impossible to say what course he had steered. Columbus stood back, therefore, for Cuba, to finish the exploring of its coast; but he no longer possessed his usual serenity of mind and unity of purpose, and was embarrassed in the prosecution of his discoveries by doubts of the designs of Pinzon. . . .

". . . Speaking in his letters to the sovereigns . . . in his artless but enthusiastic language, 'The amenity of this river, and the clearness of the water, through which the sand at the bottom may be seen; the multitude of palm-trees of various forms, the highest and most beautiful that I have met with, and an infinity of other great and green trees; the birds in rich plumage and the verdure of the fields, render this country, most serene princes, of such marvellous beauty, that it surpasses all others in charms and graces, as the day doth the night in lustre. For which reason I often say to my people, that, much as I endeavor to give a complete account of it to your majesties, my tongue cannot express the whole truth, nor my pen describe it; and I have been so overwhelmed at the sight of so much beauty, that I have not known how to relate it.' . . .

CAPTAIN ALONZO PINZON.

". . . At eleven o'clock at night, being Christmas eve . . . Columbus, who had hitherto kept watch, finding the sea calm and smooth, and the ship almost motionless, retired to rest, not having slept the preceding night. He was, in general, extremely wakeful on his coasting voyages, passing whole nights upon deck in all weathers; never trusting to the watchfulness of others, where there was any difficulty or danger to be provided against. . . .

Success Depends on Character

"No sooner had he retired than the steersman gave the helm in charge to one of the ship-boys, and went to sleep. This was in direct violation of an invariable order of the admiral, that the helm should never be intrusted to the boys. The rest of the mariners who had the watch took like advantage of the absence of Columbus, and in a little while the whole crew was buried in sleep. In the mean time the treacherous currents which run swiftly along this coast carried the vessel quietly, but with force, upon a sand-bank. The heedless boy had not noticed the breakers, although they made a roaring noise that might have been heard a league. No sooner, however, did he hear the rudder strike, and hear the tumult of the rushing sea, than he began to cry for aid. Columbus, whose careful thoughts never permitted him to sleep profoundly, was the first on deck. The master of the ship, whose duty it was to have been on watch, next made his appearance, followed by others of the crew, half awake. . . .

"It was too late to save the ship, the current having set her more upon the bank. The admiral, seeing that his boat had deserted him, that the ship had swung across the stream, and that the water was continually gaining upon her, ordered the mast to be cut away, in the hope of lightening her sufficiently to float her off. Every effort was in vain. The keel was firmly bedded in the sand; the shock had opened several seams; while the swell of the breakers, striking her broadside, left her each moment more and more aground, until she fell over on one side. Fortunately the weather continued calm, otherwise the ship must have gone to pieces, and the whole crew might have perished amid the currents and breakers. . . .

"It was on the 4th of January that Columbus set sail from La Navidad on his return to Spain. The wind being light, it was necessary to tow the caravel out of the harbor, and clear of the reefs. . . . they were detained for two days in a large bay to the west of the promontory. On the 6th they again made sail with a land breeze . . . At this time a sailor, stationed at the masthead to look out for rocks, cried out that he beheld the Pinta at a distance. The certainty of the fact gladdened

New Challenge

the heart of the admiral, and had an animating effect throughout the ship; for it was a joyful event to the mariners once more to meet with their comrades, and to have a companion bark in their voyage through these lonely seas.

"The Pinta came sweeping toward them, directly before the wind. The admiral was desirous of having a conversation with Martin Alonzo Pinzon, and seeing that all attempt was fruitless from the obstinacy of the adverse wind, and that there was no safe anchorage in the neighborhood, he put back to the bay a little west of Monte Christi, whither he was followed by the Pinta. On their first interview, Pinzon endeavored to excuse his desertion, alleging that he had been compelled to part company by stress of weather, and had ever since been seeking to rejoin the admiral. Columbus listened passively but dubiously to his apologies; and the suspicions he had conceived appeared to be warranted by subsequent information. He was told that Pinzon had been excited by accounts given him by one of the Indians on board of his vessel of a region to the eastward, abounding in gold. Taking advantage, therefore, of the superior sailing of his vessel, he had worked to windward, when the other ships had been obliged to put back, and had sought to be the first to discover and enjoy this golden region. After separating from his companions he had been entangled for several days among a cluster of small islands, supposed to have been the Caicos, but had at length been guided by the Indians to Hispaniola. Here he remained three weeks, trading with the natives in the river already mentioned, and collected a considerable quantity of gold, one half of which he retained as captain, the rest he divided among his men to secure their fidelity and secrecy.

"Such were the particulars privately related to Columbus; who, however, repressed his indignation at this flagrant breach of duty, being unwilling to disturb the remainder of his voyage with any altercations with Pinzon, who had a powerful party of relatives and townsmen in the armament. To such a degree, however, was his confidence in his confederates impaired, that he determined to return forthwith to Spain, though, under other circumstances, he would have been tempted to explore the coast in hopes of freighting his ships with treasure. . . .

". . . A little beyond this they anchored in a bay, or rather gulf, three leagues in breadth, and *Indian Encounter* extending so far inland that Columbus at first supposed it an arm of the sea, separating Hispaniola from some other land. On landing they found the natives quite different from the gentle and pacific people hitherto met with on this island. They were of a ferocious aspect, and hideously painted. Their hair was long, tied behind, and decorated with the feathers of parrots and other birds of gaudy plumage. Some were armed with war-clubs; others had bows of the length of those used by the English archers, with arrows of slender reeds, pointed with hard wood, or tipped with bone or the tooth of a fish. Their swords were of palm-wood, as hard and heavy as iron; not sharp, but broad, nearly of the thickness of two fingers, and capable, with one blow, of cleaving through a helmet to the very brains. Though thus prepared for combat, they made no attempt to molest the Spaniards; on the contrary, they sold them two of their bows and several of their arrows, and one of them was prevailed upon to go on board of the admiral's ship. . . .

"Having regaled the warrior, and made him various presents, the admiral sent him on shore . . . As the boat approached the land, upward of fifty savages, armed with bows and arrows, war-clubs, and javelins, were seen lurking among the trees. On a word from the Indian who was in the boat, they laid by their arms and came forth to meet the Spaniards. The latter, according to directions from the admiral, endeavored to purchase several of their weapons, to take as curiosities to Spain. They parted with two of their bows; but, suddenly conceiving some distrust, or thinking to overpower this handful of strangers, they rushed to the place where they had left their weapons, snatched them up, and returned with cords, as if to bind the Spaniards. The latter immediately attacked them, wounded two, put the rest to flight, and would have pursued them, but were restrained by the pilot who commanded the boat. This was the first contest with the Indians, and the first time that native blood was shed by the white men in the new world. Columbus was grieved to see all his exertions to maintain an amicable intercourse vain; he consoled himself with the idea, however, that if these were Caribs, or frontier Indians of warlike character, they would be inspired with a dread of the force and weapons of the white men, and be deterred from molesting the little garrison of Fort Nativity . . .

"Their frank and bold spirit was evidenced on the day after the skirmish, when a multitude appearing on the beach, the admiral sent a large party, well armed, on shore in the boat. The natives approached as freely and confidently as if nothing had happened; neither did they betray, throughout their subsequent intercourse, any signs of lurking fear or enmity. . . .

"Their frank and confiding conduct, so indicative of a brave and generous nature, was properly appreciated by Columbus; he received the cacique cordially, set before him a collation such as the caravel afforded, particularly biscuits and honey, which were great dainties with the Indians, and after showing him the wonders of the vessel, and making him and his attendants many presents, sent them to land highly gratified. . . .

Return Voyage
"The trade-winds which had been so propitious to Columbus on his outward voyage, were equally adverse to him on his return. The favorable breeze soon died away, and throughout the remainder of January there was a prevalence of light winds from the eastward, which prevented any great progress. . . . The weather continued mild and pleasant, and the sea so calm, that the Indians whom they were taking to Spain would frequently plunge into the water and swim about the ships. . . .

"On the 12th of February, as they were flattering themselves with soon coming in sight of land, the wind came on to blow violently, with a heavy sea; they still kept their course to the east, but with great labor and peril . . . As the morning dawned of the 14th, there was a transient pause, and they made a little sail; but the wind rose again from the south with redoubled vehemence, raging throughout the day, and increasing in fury in the night . . . For three days they lay to, with just sail enough to keep them above the waves; but the tempest still augmenting, they were obliged again to scud before the wind. The Pinta was soon lost sight of in the darkness of the night. The admiral kept as much as possible to the north-east, to approach the coast of Spain, and made signal lights at the masthead for the Pinta to do the same, and to keep in company. . . .

". . . As the day dawned the sea presented a frightful waste of wild broken waves, lashed into fury by the gale; he looked round anxiously for the Pinta, but she was nowhere to be seen. He now made a little sail, to keep his vessel ahead of the sea, lest its huge waves should break over her. As the sun rose, the wind and the waves rose with it, and throughout a dreary day the helpless bark was driven along by the fury of the tempest. . . .

"During this long and awful conflict of the elements, the mind of Columbus was a prey to the most distressing anxiety. He feared that the Pinta had foundered in the storm. In such case the whole history of his discovery, the secret of the New World depended upon his own feeble bark, and one surge of the ocean might bury it forever in oblivion. . . .

"In the midst of these gloomy apprehensions, an expedient suggested itself, by which, though he and his ship should perish, the glory of his achievement might survive to his name, and its advantages be secured to his sovereigns. He wrote on parchment a brief account of his voyage and discovery, and of his having taken possession of the newly-found lands in the name of their Catholic majesties. This he sealed and directed to the king and queen; superscribing a promise of a thousand ducats to whomsoever should deliver the packet unopened. He then wrapped it in a waxed cloth, which he placed in the centre of a cake of wax, and inclosing the whole in a large barrel, threw it into the sea . . . Lest this memorial should never reach the land he inclosed a copy in a similar manner, and placed it upon the poop, so that, should the caravel be swallowed up by the waves, the barrel might float off and survive. . . .

100

Sighting Land

"On the morning of the 15th, at daybreak, the cry of land was given ... The transports of the crew, at once more gaining sight of the Old World, were almost equal to those experienced on first beholding the New. . . . A nearer approach proved it to be an island; it was but five leagues distant, and the voyagers were congratulating themselves upon the assurance of speedily being in port, when the wind veered again . . .

"For two days they hovered in sight of the island . . . On the evening of the 17th they approached so near the first island as to cast anchor, but parting their cable, had to put to sea again, where they remained beating about until the following morning, when they anchored under the shelter of its northern side. For several days Columbus had been in such a state of agitation and anxiety as scarcely to take food or repose. Although suffering greatly from a gouty affection to which he was subject, yet he had maintained his watchful post on deck, exposed to wintry cold, to the pelting of the storm, and the drenching surges of the sea. It was not until the night of the 17th that he got a little sleep, more from the exhaustion of nature than from any tranquillity of mind. Such were the difficulties and perils which attended his return to Europe; had one tenth part of them beset his outward voyage, his timid and factious crew would have risen in arms against the enterprise, and he never would have discovered the New World. . . .

Difficulties in Portugal

"On the following morning Columbus reminded his people of their vow to perform a pious procession at the first place where they should land. . . .

"An ungenerous reception, however, awaited the poor tempest-tossed mariners on their first return to the abode of civilized men, far different from the sympathy and hospitality they had experienced among the savages of the New World. Scarcely had they begun their prayers and thanksgivings, when the rabble of the village, horse and foot, headed by the governor, surrounded the hermitage and took them all prisoners. . . .

"The King of Portugal, jealous lest the expedition of Columbus might interfere with his own discoveries, had sent orders to his commanders of islands and distant ports to seize and detain him whenever he should be met with. . . . Such was the first reception of the admiral on his return to the Old World, an earnest of the crosses and troubles with which he was to be requited throughout life, for one of the greatest benefits that ever man conferred upon his fellow-beings. . . .

Success

". . . The king, with his usual magnificence, issued orders . . . that everything which the admiral required for himself, his crew or his vessel, should be furnished promptly and abundantly, without cost.

"Columbus would gladly have declined the royal invitation, feeling distrust of the good faith of the king; but tempestuous weather had placed him in his power, and he thought it prudent to avoid all appearance of suspicion. . . .

"On approaching the royal residence, the principal cavaliers of the king's household came forth to meet him, and attended him with great ceremony to the palace. His reception by the monarch was worthy of an enlightened prince. He ordered him to seat himself in his presence, an honor only granted to persons of royal dignity; and after many congratulations on the result of his enterprise, assured him that everything in his kingdom that could be of service to his sovereigns or himself was at his command.

". . . Columbus gave an account of his voyage, and of the countries he had discovered. The king listened with much seeming pleasure, but with secret grief and mortification; reflecting that this splendid enterprise had once been offered to himself, and had been rejected. A casual observation showed what was passing in his thoughts. He expressed a doubt whether the discovery did not really appertain to the crown of Portugal, according to the capitulations of the treaty of 1479 with the Castilian sovereigns. Columbus replied that he had never seen those capitulations, nor knew anything of their nature . . . The king made a gracious reply, expressing himself satisfied that he had acted correctly, and persuaded that these matters would be readily adjusted between the two powers, without the need of umpires. . . .

"On suggesting these doubts to his councillors, they eagerly confirmed them. Some of these were the very persons who had once derided this enterprise, and scoffed at Columbus as a dreamer. To them its success was a source of confusion; and the return of Columbus, covered with glory, a deep humiliation. . . . Seeing the king much perturbed in spirit, some even went so far as to propose, as a means of impeding the prosecution of these enterprises, that Columbus should be assassinated; declaring that he deserved death for attempting to deceive and embroil the two nations by his pretended discoveries. . . .

"Happily, the king had too much magnanimity to adopt the iniquitous measure proposed. He did justice to the great merit of Columbus, and honored him as a distinguished benefactor of mankind; and he felt it his duty, as a generous prince, to protect all strangers driven by adverse fortune to his ports. . . .

Enterprise Accomplished "The triumphant return of Columbus was a prodigious event in the history of the little port of Palos, where everybody was more or less interested in the fate of his expedition. The most important and wealthy sea-captains of the place had engaged in it, and scarcely a family but had some relative or friend among the navigators. The departure of the ships upon what appeared a chimerical and desperate cruise, had spread gloom and dismay over the place; and the storms which had raged throughout the winter had heightened the public despondency. . . .

"Great was the agitation of the inhabitants, therefore, when they beheld one of the ships standing up the river; but when they learned that she returned in triumph from the discovery of a world, the whole community broke forth in transports of joy. The bells were rung, the shops shut, all business was suspended: for a time there was nothing but hurry and tumult.

When Columbus landed the multitude thronged to see and welcome him, and a grand procession was formed to the principal church, to return thanks to God for so signal a discovery made by the people of that place—forgetting, in their exultation, the thousand difficulties they had thrown in the way of the enterprise. Wherever Columbus passed, he was hailed with shouts and acclamations. What a contrast to his departure a few months before, followed by murmurs and execrations; or, rather, what a contrast to his first arrival at Palos, a poor pedestrian, craving bread and water for his child at the gate of a convent! . . .

"It is a singular coincidence . . . that on the very evening of the arrival of Columbus at Palos . . . the Pinta, commanded by Martin Alonzo Pinzon, likewise entered the river. After her separation from the admiral in the storm, she had been driven before the gale into the Bay of Biscay, and had made the port of Bayonne. Doubting whether Columbus had survived the tempest, Pinzon had immediately written to the sovereigns giving information of the discovery he had made, and had requested permission to come to court and communicate the particulars in person. As soon as the weather permitted, he had again set sail, anticipating a triumphant reception in his native port of Palos. When, on entering the harbor, he beheld the vessel of the admiral riding at anchor, and learnt the enthusiasm with which he had been received, the heart of Pinzon died within him. It is said that he feared to meet Columbus in this hour of his triumph, lest he should put him under arrest for his desertion on the coast of Cuba; but he was a man of too much resolution to indulge in such a fear. It is more probable that consciousness of his misconduct made him unwilling to appear before the public in the midst of their enthusiasm for Columbus, and perhaps he sickened at the honors heaped upon Columbus as so many reproaches on himself. The reply of the sovereigns to his letter at length arrived. It was of a reproachful tenor, and forbade his appearance at court. This letter completed his humiliation; the anguish of his feelings gave virulence to his bodily malady, and in a few days he died, a victim to deep chagrin.

"Let no one, however, indulge in harsh censures over the grave of Pinzon! His merits and services are entitled to the highest praise; his errors should be regarded with indulgence. He was one of the foremost in Spain to appreciate the project of Columbus, animating him by his concurrence and aiding him with his purse, when poor and unknown at Palos. He afterward enabled him to procure and fit out ships, when even the mandates of the sovereigns were ineffectual; and finally embarked in the expedition with his brothers and his friends, staking life, property, everything upon the event. He thus entitled himself to participate largely in the glory of this immortal enterprise; but unfortunately, forgetting for a moment the grandeur of the cause, and the implicit obedience due to his commander, he yielded to the incitements of self-interest, and committed that act of insubordination which has cast a shade upon his name. In extenuation of his fault, however, may be alleged his habits of command, which rendered him impatient of control; his consciousness of having rendered great services to the expedition, and of possessing property in the ships. That he was a man of great professional merit is admitted by all his contemporaries; that he naturally possessed generous sentiments and an honorable ambition, is evident from the poignancy with which he felt the disgrace drawn on him by his misconduct. A mean man would not have fallen a victim to self-upbraiding for having been convicted of a mean action. His story shows how one lapse from duty may counterbalance the merits of a thousand services; how one moment of weakness may mar the beauty of a whole life of virtue; and how important it is for a man, under all circumstances, to be true not merely to others, but to himself. . . .

Esteem and Honor
"The fame of his discovery had resounded throughout the nation, and as his route lay through several of the finest and most populous provinces of Spain, his journey appeared like the progress of a sovereign. . . .

"About the middle of April Columbus arrived at Barcelona, where every preparation had been made to give him a solemn and magnificent reception. . . . It seemed as if the public eye could not be sated with gazing on these trophies of an unknown world; or on the remarkable man by whom it had been discovered. There was a sublimity in this event that mingled a solemn feeling with the public joy. It was looked upon as a vast and signal dispensation of Providence, in reward for the piety of the monarchs; and the majestic and venerable appearance of the discoverer, so different from the youth and buoyancy generally expected from roving enterprise, seemed in harmony with the grandeur and dignity of his achievement.

"To receive him with suitable pomp and distinction, the sovereigns had ordered their throne to be placed in public under a rich canopy of brocade of gold . . . Here the king and queen awaited his arrival, seated in state . . . and attended by the dignitaries of their court, and the principal nobility of Castile, Valentia, Catalonia, and Arragon, all impatient to behold the man who had conferred so incalculable a benefit upon the nation. At length Columbus entered the hall, surrounded by a brilliant crowd of cavaliers, among whom . . . he was conspicuous for his stately and commanding person, which with his countenance, rendered venerable by his gray hairs, gave him the august appearance of a senator of Rome; a modest smile lighted up his features, showing that he enjoyed the state and glory in which he came; and certainly nothing could be more deeply moving to a mind inflamed by noble ambition, and conscious of having greatly deserved, than these testimonials of the admiration and gratitude of a nation, or rather of a world. As Columbus approached the sovereigns rose, as if receiving a person of the highest rank. Bending his knees, he offered to kiss their hands; but there was some hesitation on their part to permit this act of homage. Raising him in the most gracious manner, they ordered him to seat himself in their presence; a rare honor in this proud and punctilious court.

"At their request he now gave an account of the most striking events of his voyage, and a description of the islands discovered. . . .

"When he had finished, the sovereigns sank on their knees, and raising their clasped hands to heaven, their eyes filled with tears of joy and gratitude, poured forth thanks and praises to God for so great a providence; all present followed their example; a deep and solemn enthusiasm pervaded that splendid assembly, and prevented all common acclamations of triumph. . . . Such was the solemn and pious manner in which the brilliant court of Spain celebrated this sublime event; offering up a grateful tribute of melody and praise, and giving glory to God for the discovery of another world. . . .

America "The joy occasioned by the great discovery of Columbus was not confined to Spain; the tidings were spread far and wide by the communications of ambassadors, the correspondence of the learned, the negotiations of merchants, and the reports of travellers, and the whole civilized world was filled with wonder and delight . . . The news was brought to Genoa and was recorded among the triumphant events of the year; for the republic, though she may have slighted the opportunity of making herself mistress of the discovery, has ever since been tenacious of the glory of having given birth to the discoverer. The tidings were soon carried to England, which as yet was but a maritime power of inferior importance. They caused, however, much wonder in London, and great talk and admiration in the court of Henry VII., where the discovery was pronounced 'a thing more divine than human.' We have this on the authority of Sebastian Cabot himself, the future

discoverer of the northern continent of America, who was in London at the time, and was inspired by the event with a generous spirit of emulation.

"Every member of civilized society, in fact, rejoiced in the occurrence, as one in which he was more or less interested. To some it opened a new and unbounded field of inquiry; to others, of enterprise; and every one awaited with intense eagerness the further development of this unknown world, still covered with mystery, the partial glimpses of which were so full of wonder. . . .

"During the whole of his sojourn at Barcelona, the sovereigns took every occasion to bestow on Columbus personal marks of their high consideration. He was admitted at all times to the royal presence, and the queen delighted to converse with him on the subject of his enterprises. . . . To perpetuate in his family the glory of his achievement, a coat of arms was assigned him, in which the royal arms, the castle and lion, were quartered with his proper bearings, which were a group of islands surrounded by waves. To these arms was afterward annexed the motto:

To Castile and Leon
Columbus gave a new world."[23]

THE ARMS OF COLUMBUS.
(Containing the castle of Castile, the lion of Arragon, the anchors of a sea captain and the islands of a discoverer.)

Illustrations: The illustrations included in this selection from *The Life and Voyages of Christopher Columbus* are taken from *The True Story of Christopher Columbus,* by Elbridge S. Brooks, 1892.

APPENDIX

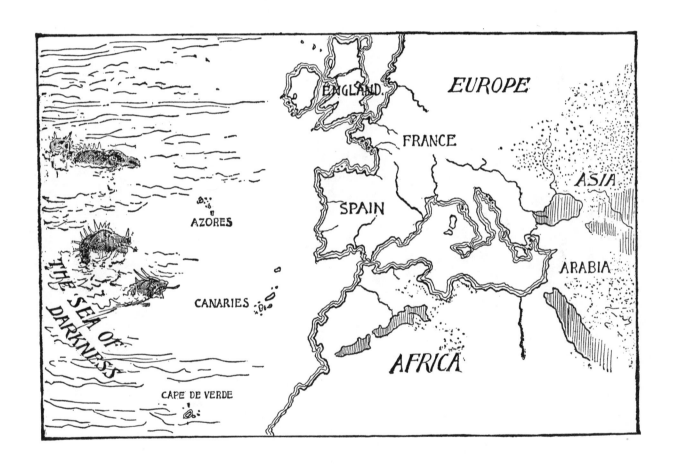

THE WORLD AS COLUMBUS KNEW IT WHEN HE WENT TO SCHOOL.

SUGGESTED STUDENT ACTIVITIES

The activities suggested here are appropriate for teaching either biography. These activities should not be repeated for students who study both biographies in consecutive years. In a school setting, the teacher should determine which activities are most appropriate for each grade level. Certain activities would be enjoyable for both grade levels to do together as a joint project.

1. Find pictures of sailors using the compass, sun, and stars to find their way. Compare travelling by land and sea so that the children understand how much more difficult sailing is.

2. Bring some spices to class for the students to observe the great variety of tastes and smells. Help them understand how spices make food taste better, and why the Europeans wanted them so much.

3. Find a clear picture of Ferdinand and Isabella's coat of arms for the students to color or cut and paste.

4. Find a large map of Spain. Identify how far Columbus had to travel.

5. If possible, find a way for the children to take pony rides and compare how much longer it took to travel by a mule or on horseback than it does today to travel in a car or by airplane.

6. Find pictures of the Nina, Pinta, and Santa Maria to show students. If possible, prepare a model for them to look at and pictures for them to color.

7. If possible, take the children to look at some sailing vessels. Try to compare the size of Columbus's ships to the size of ships today.

8. Sing appropriate songs about sailing.

9. Take the students outside and point out the horizon to them.

10. Prepare an outdoor activity for the students. Place objects on the ground or up in the trees to represent the signs which encouraged the sailors that land was near—carved stick, leaves, flowers, birds, and a glimmering light. Each day, have the students go outside and search for the clues which were included in that day's lesson. Have a treat for the students to enjoy once they have arrived on land.

11. Count the number of days it took to make the voyage.

12. Prepare a picture of a ship. Using string and construction paper have the students cut out an anchor and glue the "rope and anchor" on the picture to represent dropping the anchor.

13. Use pictures of gold-mines to show the students how the gold had to be found and mined.

14. Prepare a re-enactment of Columbus's parade before the King and Queen of Spain. Write a simple script for Columbus, Queen Isabella, King Ferdinand, and possibly the King of Portugal. Use imagination in making it an

enjoyable and memorable event. Students may wish to invite their parents to attend the festivity.

15. Introduce the students to the plants and animals of South America.
  • Visit the library for books, videos, or other resources identifying the unique South American plants and animals.

  • Visit a zoo or pet store to see parrots and other South American animals.

  • Find pictures of parrots for the students to color or make a parrot out of colored construction paper.

SAMPLE TEST QUESTIONS

When teaching a biography to students who are able to read and write sentence answers, frequent, short tests may be given at appropriate intervals throughout the study. The teacher must consider carefully the number and type of questions in relationship to the abilities of the students. First grade students should be able to answer two or three questions which require reasoning and sentence answers.

Tests are intended to evaluate the student's understanding of the material presented and ability to reason regarding that information. Therefore, test questions should relate specifically to the leading ideas which have been taught. Consistent review of these ideas will assure that the students comprehend the material presented, and they should be able to take a test without memorizing their notes or studying lists of review questions.

Following are a variety of sample test questions which may be used with either biography of Columbus in a class of students who can read and write. The teacher may wish to revise these questions appropriately to correspond to the leading ideas emphasized in class.

  • What special plan did God have for Columbus's life?

  • Describe three different ways God prepared Columbus to fulfill His plan.

  • Identify two character qualities which helped Columbus succeed. Give an example from his life for each.

  • How was God's plan for Columbus even better than finding a path to the Indies?

  • What lesson can be learned from the difficulties Columbus faced in his life?

  • Why was Columbus able to stay strong even when the men were discouraged?

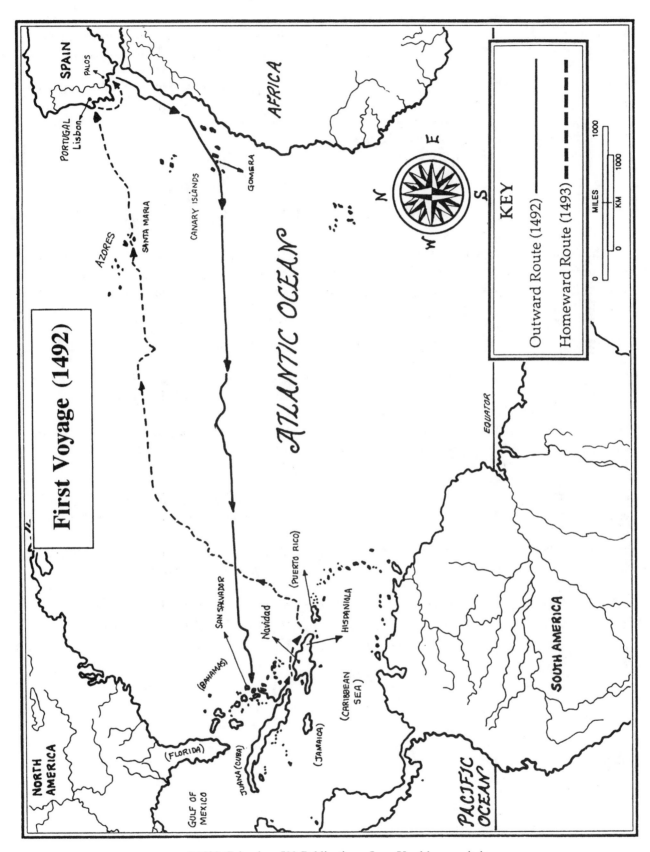

First Voyage (1492)

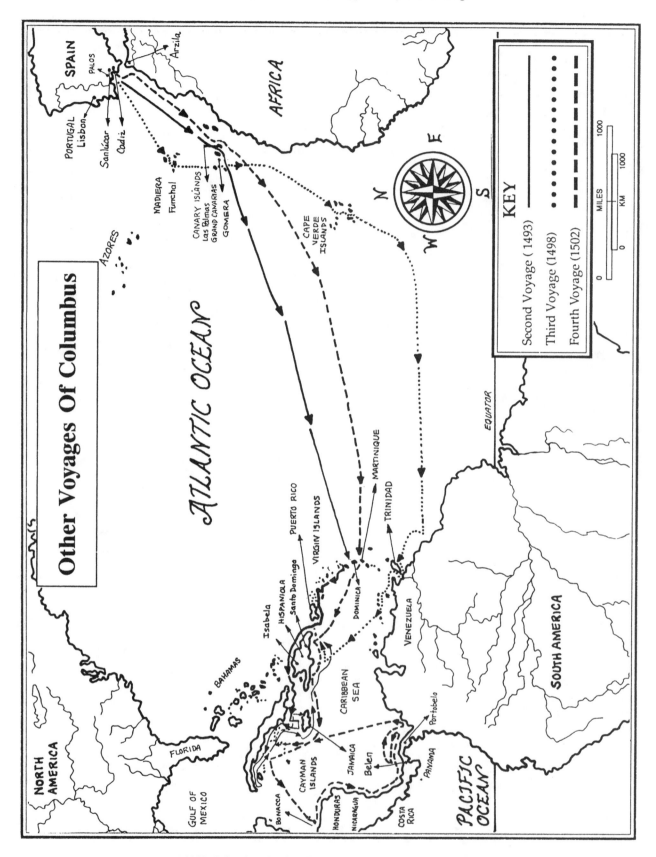

Other Voyages Of Columbus

KEY

Second Voyage (1493)
Third Voyage (1498)
Fourth Voyage (1502)

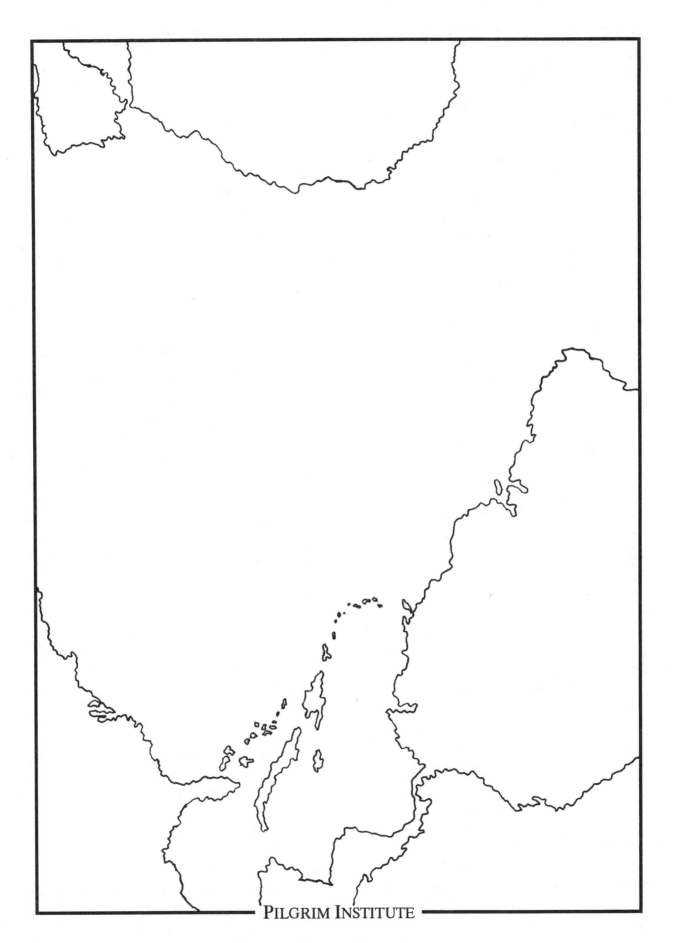

PILGRIM INSTITUTE

ENDNOTES

1. Psalm 78:6-7.

2. Emma Willard, "History of the United States, or Republic of America," *The Christian History of the Constitution of the United States of America*, Verna M. Hall, Compiler, (San Francisco: Foundation for American Christian Education, 1966), p. 405.

3. Rev. S. W. Foljambe, "The Hand of God in American History," *The Christian History of the American Revolution*, Verna M. Hall, Compiler, (San Francisco: Foundation for American Christian Education, 1975), p. 47a.

4. Rev. S. W. Foljambe, ibid., p. 46b.

5. Ruth J. Smith, "Teaching America's Christian History in the Elementary School," *A Guide to American Christian Education for the Home and School*, by James B. Rose, (Palo Cedro, California: American Christian History Institute, 1987), pp. 201-227.

6. Verna M. Hall, *The Christian History of the Constitution of the United States of America*, (San Francisco: Foundation for American Christian Education, 1966), p. 6A.

7. Kay Brigham, Trans., *Christopher Columbus's Book of Prophecies*, by Christopher Columbus, (Fort Lauderdale, Florida: TSELF, Inc., 1992), p. 173-183.

8. Verna M. Hall, *The Christian History of the American Revolution*, (San Francisco: Foundation for American Christian Education, 1975), p. xxv.

9. Verna M. Hall, ibid., pp. 47-48.

10. Ruth J. Smith, op. cit., p. 204.

11. Rosalie J. Slater, *Teaching and Learning America's Christian History*, (San Francisco: Foundation for American Christian Education, 1965), pp. 113-136.

12. Rosalie J. Slater, *A Family Program for Reading Aloud*, (San Francisco: Foundation for American Christian Education, 1991). p. 25-26.

13. Ibid., pp. 113-117.

14. Slater, *Teaching and Learning America's Christian History*, op. cit., p. 155.

15. Ibid., p. 3-4.

16. Fernando Colon, *The Life of the Admiral Christopher Columbus, by his son, Ferdinand*, (New Brunswick, N.J.: Rutgers University Press, 1959) p. 4.

17. William Bradford, "Of Plimoth Plantation," *The Christian History of the Constitution of the United States of America*, Verna M. Hall, Compiler, (San Francisco: Foundation for American Christian Education, 1966), pp. 193-194.

18. Joaquin Miller, "Columbus."

19. James T. deKay, *Meet Christopher Columbus*, (New York: Random House, 1968).

20. Charles Bancroft, "Footprints of Time," *The Christian History of the Constitution of the United States of America*, Verna M. Hall, Compiler, (San Francisco: Foundation for American Christian Education, 1966), p. 8.

21. Long, William J., *American Literature*, (Chicago: Ginn and Company, 1923), p. 179.

22. Washington Irving, *The Life and Voyages of Christopher Columbus*, (Chicago: Hooper, Clarke & Co.), Volume I, p. 14.

23. Ibid.

BIBLIOGRAPHY

Brigham, Kay, Trans. *Christopher Columbus's Book of Prophecies*, by Christopher Columbus. Fort Lauderdale: TSELF, Inc., 1992.

Colon, Fernando. *The Life of the Admiral Christopher Columbus, by his son, Ferdinand.* New Brunswick: Rutgers University Press, 1959.

Hall, Verna M. *The Christian History of the American Revolution: Consider and Ponder.* San Francisco: Foundation for American Christian Education, 1976.

_____. *The Christian History of the Constitution of the United States of America.* San Francisco: Foundation for American Christian Education, 1966.

Hall, Verna M., and Rosalie J. Slater. *Rudiments of America's Christian History and Government.* San Francisco: Foundation for American Christian Education, 1968.

Irving, Washington. *The Life and Voyages of Christopher Columbus.* Chicago: Hooper, Clarke & Co.

Long, William J. *American Literature.* Chicago: Ginn and Company, 1923.

Morison, Samuel Eliot. *Admiral of the Ocean Sea.* Boston: Little, Brown, and Company, 1942.

_____. *Journals and Other Documents on the Life and Voyages of Christopher Columbus.* New York: The Heritage Press, 1963.

Old South Leaflets. Boston: The Old South Association.

Slater, Rosalie J. *Teaching and Learning America's Christian History.* San Francisco: Foundation for American Christian Education, 1965.

Slater, Rosalie J. *A Family Program for Reading Aloud.* San Francisco: Foundation for American Christian Education, 1991.

Smith, Ruth J. "Teaching America's Christian History in the Elementary School." *A Guide to American Christian Education for the Home and School,* by James B. Rose. Palo Cedro: American Christian History Institute, 1987.

FOR FURTHER UNDERSTANDING OF AN AMERICAN CHRISTIAN PHILOSOPHY OF HISTORY, GOVERNMENT, AND EDUCATION

THE PILGRIM INSTITUTE

The Pilgrim Institute was established in 1979 to preserve America's Providential History and to restore American Christian Education. Believing that our nation can be restored through the teaching and living of the Biblical principles upon which the nation was built, Pilgrim Institute offers a continuing training program for individuals who desire to reclaim their American Christian history, and relate a Biblical philosophy of government to every aspect of their lives. This educational program embraces pastors, Christian school educators, home school educators, businessmen, and laymen in their unique responsibility for restoring America to the practice of self-government, individually and civilly.

INSTITUTE PROGRAM

- *Introductory Seminars* - Two days in length, present the ideas that America has a Christian history and the need for American Christians to understand the Biblical foundation of our nation and help to restore it.
- *Regional Conferences* - Offers two levels of training — introductory and advanced. The American Christian philosophy of history and government is related to the home, the church, the marketplace, and the school.
- *Rudiments of America's Christian History and Government* - A basic training course offered in two formats — a one-week course and an audio correspondence course. This course assists the American Christian in developing a knowledge of America's Christian history and her Christian form of government. The method of the Principle Approach applies to all areas of life — the home, church, classroom, and civil government.
- *Advanced Training Courses* - Offered in one and two-week sessions, and by correspondence, these courses provide advanced training in America's Christian History and Government, Administration, and specific subject areas, i.e., Literature, Grammar, Universal History, etc.

- *Consultation Service* - Assists school administrators in developing the training program for faculty, parents, and students to implement the American Christian philosophy of history, government, and education.
- *American Christian Master Teacher Program* - A mutual ministry with the American Christian History Institute of Palo Cedro, California, involves enlisting and training qualified individuals to be Master Teachers of America's Christian history, government, and education.

TEACHING AMERICA'S CHRISTIAN HISTORY IN THE ELEMENTARY SCHOOL

American Christian Education requires the parent/teacher to prepare himself internally to teach America's Christian History in the elementary school through his development of a Biblical philosophy of history and government. Such preparation comes by reasoning, relating, and recording the explicit evidence of those Biblical principles and key links advanced by the Hand of God on the Chain of Christianity. Ruth J. Smith has developed a suggested program for *Teaching America's Christian History in the Elementary School,* published in *A Guide to American Christian Education for the Home and School.* A series of *Guides* are being developed to further assist the parent/teacher in teaching America's Christian history to elementary students.

An American Christian Approach for Teaching CHRISTOPHER COLUMBUS AND THE DISCOVERY OF THE NEW WORLD *by Lynn M. Meier and Ruth J. Smith*

Direction for teaching Josephine Pollard's biography, *Christopher Columbus and the Discovery of the New World,* is given in this *Teaching Guide* for the upper elementary grades.

In addition to discerning the remarkable character of the great discoverer, Josephine Pollard's biography presents specific acts of Providence, examples of the justice of God, and the vast treasures of the New World waiting to be developed. The *Guide* assists the teacher in discerning cause and effect relationships, the various forms of government which could have been planted and why God's choice was best, and the Biblical principles of America's Christian History and Government. Specific suggestions are made for student work, research projects, timelines, maps, interesting class activities, and bulletin boards. "His trust in God, and his faith in himself, brought Columbus through straits which would have crushed a man less brave and bold." The lessons of this book are the timeless lessons of life which may be planted in the hearts of your students.

Paperbound

Suggested grade level 4-6

CHRISTOPHER COLUMBUS
AND THE
Discovery of the New World
by Josephine Pollard

Masterful literary quality and a depth of timeless truths provide a top quality biography for students in the upper elementary grades. Among many other leading ideas, the students will see how God prepares individuals and then He causes events. "Columbus wove the chain that links the old world to the new . . . the tale has for us a fresh charm, and old and young find in it some new thought to dwell upon." (Preface)

Paperbound

NOAH WEBSTER
Father of the Dictionary
by Isabel Proudfit

Noah Webster is rightly called "the father of American Christian education." He established America's independence in education by applying the principle approach to spelling, language, and literature. Some 25 million copies of his "Blue-Backed Speller" were used in America's schools during his life-time. However, Webster's American Dictionary of the English language was his greatest achievement; in it he made copious use of the Scriptures as a basic reference source.

Reprint Anticipated

OTHER PUBLICATIONS

RESTORING AMERICA'S HERITAGE
OF
PASTORAL LEADERSHIP
by Glen Jaspers and Ruth J. Smith

This manual is designed to introduce the individual pastor, educator, or layman to America's Christian history and a Biblical philosophy of government and education. The manual includes references, along with leading questions, to direct research in the basic volumes of America's Christian History published by the Foundation for American Christian Education.

Loose-Leaf

For further information on Pilgrim Institute Program or Publications, Contact:
THE PILGRIM INSTITUTE
P. O. Box 454 ● Granger, Indiana 46530

AMERICAN CHRISTIAN HISTORY INSTITUTE

A GUIDE TO AMERICAN CHRISTIAN EDUCATION
FOR THE HOME AND SCHOOL
THE PRINCIPLE APPROACH
by James B. Rose

The *Guide* provides an in-depth, detailed and historical explanation of the Principle Approach and of "how to think governmentally" from a Biblical perspective. It breaks out the principles of America's Christian history; shows how they apply to life and living; provides direction in how to teach America's Christian history and government; includes charts, diagrams, and Biblical index to explain the Principle Approach and how to apply it to the Home, School-at-Home, and to the Kindergarten, Elementary and High School Curriculum. A 550-page book, cranberry vellum, gold-stamped with Eagle's nest embossed.

STUDY GUIDE
by Mary-Elaine Swanson
TO
THE CHRISTIAN HISTORY OF THE CONSTITUTION
OF THE UNITED STATES OF AMERICA:
CHRISTIAN SELF-GOVERNMENT WITH UNION
Compiled by Verna M. Hall

A Guide to lead students through *Christian Self-Government with Union*, Volume II, and to discover the importance of "first principles" to our Founding Fathers, the leadership of the colonial clergy, and the tactics and methods of Christian resistance to British tyranny during the "Decade of Debate" (1765-1775) with the remarkable spirit of Christian unity that developed over this period. Paperbound

PHYSICAL GEOGRAPHY
by Arnold Guyot

A reprint of the 1873 edition of *Physical Geography* by Arnold Guyot, Swiss-born geographer, creation scientist, and a professor of geography and geology at Princeton University. This reprint complements the *Principle Approach to Geography* in *The Guide to American Christian Education* and is enhanced with a new Introduction by Katherine Dang, author of *Geography, An American Christian Approach,* published in the *Guide.* Paperbound

---

For Ordering Information, Contact:
THE AMERICAN CHRISTIAN HISTORY INSTITUTE
P. O. Box 648 ● Palo Cedro, CA 96073

THE FOUNDATION FOR AMERICAN CHRISTIAN EDUCATION

The two basic books, *The Christian History of the Constitution of the United States of America: Christian Self-Government* and *Teaching and Learning America's Christian History: The Principle Approach*, enable us to teach present-day American Christians the Biblical principles which established us as ONE NATION UNDER GOD.

Knowledge of God's principle of individuality, Christian self-government, property as conscience and productivity, and the Christian form of our government, enable parents and teachers to restore the PRINCIPLE APPROACH method of REASONING and WRITING in the development of Christian curriculum. America's Christian History teaches us the Providence of God in our individual lives today as well as in the life of our nation.

A Family Program for Reading Aloud for the home study of literature restores home as a teaching center and offers the primary library you need for self-education and teaching others. Reading aloud in

the family circle, based on a Biblical foundation and your study of America's Christian history, can be a major part of home education or supplement to your children's school education, and bring enhanced unity in the home. *A Family Program for Reading Aloud* by Rosalie J. Slater reviews over 200 books from pre-school through high school/adult level reading, with application to sharing these classics in historical perspective with Biblical understanding.

ILLUSTRATED AND INDEXED, FULL-COLOR COVER, 128-PAGE PAPERBACK

One of the very special books presented in *A Family Program for Reading Aloud* is *Mother Carey's Chickens,* last published in 1911 and unavailable for many decades, has just been republished by

F.A.C.E. This delightful read-aloud family story by Kate Douglas Wiggin, author of the well known *Rebecca of Sunnybrook Farm,* gives us a chronicle of family spirit-building, of mothering and rearing children, that is a beacon on the present, bleak horizon where the family as an institution is under siege. The story imparts not only timeless principles, but images to inspire real beauty and truth in family relations, in Christ-like gentleness, authority, and power. It gives us this and all the elements of a beloved, read-aloud story, full of joy and pathos, and the pulses of family life.

ILLUSTRATED, FULL-COLOR COVER, 365-PAGE PAPERBACK